conversation in
ITALIAN
points of departure

conversation in ITALIAN

points of departure

Gabriel J. Paolozzi
Grambling State University

Frank Sedwick
Rollins College

D. VAN NOSTRAND COMPANY
New York Cincinnati Toronto London Melbourne

D. VAN NOSTRAND COMPANY Regional Offices:
New York   Cincinnati   Millbrae

D. VAN NOSTRAND COMPANY International Offices:
London   Toronto   Melbourne

Published by D. VAN NOSTRAND COMPANY
450 West 33rd Street, New York, N. Y. 10001

Published simultaneously in Canada by
VAN NOSTRAND REINHOLD LTD.

10   9   8   7   6   5   4   3   2   1

Preface

Conversation in Italian: Points of Departure is designed for conversation and composition on either the intermediate or advanced level. The difference between levels will lie in the degree of sophistication of the student's responses: the advanced student should exhibit greater control of structure, more mature syntax, a richer vocabulary, a more lively imagination, and in general keener tools of self-expression.

There are fifty-one scenes, grouped arbitrarily. They cut across as many social strata and cover as many everyday necessities as possible, most of them with types of people and situations credible equally for the home country as for the country whose language the student is studying. Where differences in custom exist, many of these will be either evident in the picture itself or noted in the textual material; the instructor may well supply others.

Flexibility and simplicity are the keynote of this book. Begin anywhere. Skip around among the lessons, backward or forward, as you wish. There is no progressive degree of difficulty; no lesson depends on any other lesson; and the specific vocabulary for each scene is self-sustaining for that lesson; hence there is no need for a vocabulary at the end of the book. Omit whatever you wish. One scene and its paraphernalia, if pursued in their entirety, are sufficient preparation for a one-hour class.

Since this book is designed for use beyond the beginning level, it is assumed that students know the basic grammar and have at their command a fundamental vocabulary (although an appendix of numbers, verb tenses, and irregular verbs is useful at any level, and so included here). The commonest words are taken for granted. Though not necessary, it might be helpful if students had their own dictionaries for working from English to Italian.

The title of the book with its reference to "points of departure" suggests the expansive way in which the various scenes should be used. The repetitiousness of the pattern drill and the contrived dialog are eschewed in favor of free and inventive response to pictorial suggestion. The only novelty lies in the emphasis of the interrelationships of people and objects and situations, all as modern and universal and youth-oriented as possible and cast into a series of questions whose ultimate aim is to expand conversations from, rather than limit them to, the picture at hand.

Each lesson has a picture, a word list pertinent to that picture, a set of questions analyzing the picture, a set of "points of departure" questions utilizing the given vocabulary but not necessarily the picture, and three suggested topics for discourse.

The word list will always include three groupings in this order: (1) verbs; (2) nouns; (3) other words and expressions. Every word in the list is used somewhere in the questions or its use is occasioned somewhere in the answers.

With the exception of the common words, all questions use only the vocabulary of their own lesson, as does the simplest form of their possible replies. The questions will always total twenty, sometimes equally divided between the two types, but not always so. No question is answerable only by *yes* or *no*, though many of the first set of questions can be answered briefly. The "points of departure" questions require more thoughtful replies, in many cases rather detailed ones. Preparation of the responses to the questions may be either written or oral but should be done outside the classroom, where activity should be oral.

Additional questions will occur to the instructor as the class is in progress, for it is through spontaneous repartee that the ultimate aim of this book is accomplished.

The three topics for written or oral discourse may be corrected either orally in class or handed to the instructor for individual annotation. Each student would choose one theme, because not all of the three topics in any given lesson will appeal to or be answerable by everybody. Of the three topics, there will always be at least one which requires little imagination or linguistic accomplishment, but at least one other is calculated to challenge the ingenuity of the best student. The list of words of any given lesson will normally be sufficient to meet the needs of at least one of these themes. Themes written in the first person do not necessarily have to be true, for at all times students are urged to combine imaginative inventiveness with linguistic skills and the vocabulary at their disposal.

G.J.P.
F.S.

Indice

Avviso preliminare

Qui sotto Lei troverà un elenco di parole che appaiono con frequenza nelle lezioni seguenti, enumerate qui per evitare eccessiva ripetizione. Lei già conosce molte di queste parole. Se non le conosce, Le consigliamo di impararle ora poichè non figurano in nessuno degli elenchi seguenti. Inoltre suggeriamo che Lei studi i tempi dei verbi, i verbi irregolari più comuni ed i numeri. Tutti si trovano nell'appendice.

accadere to happen
comprare to buy
costare to cost
dedurre to deduce, to subtract
descrivere to describe
dovere should, ought
guardare to look (at)
nominare to name
pagare to pay
parere to seem, to appear
piacere to be pleasing (to like)
portare to wear (*articles of clothing*), to carry, to bear, to have
potere to be able
preferire to prefer
scegliere to choose
servire to serve, to be of use
significare to mean
sperare to hope
spiegare to explain
succedere to happen
supporre to suppose
tenere to hold, to keep
tradurre to translate
trovare, trovarsi to find, to be
usare to use

vendere to sell
vistir (si) to dress
voler dire to mean

compito task, duty
disegno picture (drawing)
genere kind, type
luogo place
oggetto object
ragione reason
somiglianza similarity
svantaggio disadvantage
vantaggio advantage

accanto a at the side of, next to
a destra on the right
a sinistra on the left
davanti a in front of
dietro in back of, behind
fino a until
in fondo in the background
in genere generally
in primo piano in the foreground
secondo according to
sopra on, above
sotto underneath, under

to telephone (to call, make a call) **telefonare**
to dial a number **formare un numero**
to make a long-distance call **fare una telefonata interurbana**
to cut off **interrompere**
to dial "direct" **telefonare direttamente, telefonare in teleselezione**
to hang up **riattaccare**
to call "collect" **fare una telefonata con addebito al numero chiamato**
to accept the charges **accettare l'addebito, accettare le spese**
to pick up (*a receiver*) **staccare**
to resort to; to ask **ricorrere a**
to wait **aspettare**
to hear **sentire**

telephone **il telefono, l'apparecchio**
receiver **il ricevitore, l'auricolare** (*m.*)
pay (public) telephone **il telefono pubblico**
long distance **la telefonata interurbana**
telephone bill **il conto del telefono**
telephone book **l'elenco telefonico**
telephone booth **la cabina telefonica**
local call **la telefonata (o chiamata) urbana**
station-to-station call **la telefonata da stazione a stazione**
person-to-person call **la telefonata da persona a persona**

operator **il (la) telefonista**
telephone number **il numero di telefono**
area code **il prefisso**
party line **la linea di ⟨⟨duplex⟩⟩**
private line **la linea privata**
dial tone **il segnale acustico**
collect call **la telefonata con addebito al numero chiamato**
switchboard **il centralino telefonico**
cord **il cordone telefonico**
digit **il numero**
minimum charge **la tariffa minima**
content **il contenuto**

sure, certain **certo, sicuro**
the line is busy **la linea è occupata**
hello! **pronto!**

Parlando per telefono

Analisi del disegno

1. Chi ha telefonato a chi? Può essere certo Lei? Perchè?
2. Da che tipo di telefono sta telefonando il ragazzo?
3. In quale mano tiene il ricevitore il ragazzo? E la ragazza? Dov'è l'altra mano del ragazzo?
4. Secondo Lei, che può essere il soggetto della conversazione?
5. Da quale parte del ricevitore esce il cordone?

Punti di partenza

6. Qual è il numero di telefono della Sua casa?
7. Quanti numeri ha il prefisso?
8. Perchè costa di più una telefonata da persona a persona che una da stazione a stazione?
9. Se non si può telefonare direttamente, a chi si ricorre per fare una telefonata interurbana?
10. Quanto costa una telefonata urbana?
11. Che cosa fa Lei generalmente se nel formare un numero la linea è occupata?
12. Che fa Lei se si interrompe la comunicazione durante una telefonata interurbana?
13. Descriva un elenco telefonico ed il suo contenuto.
14. Preferisce Lei una linea di « duplex » o una linea privata? Perchè?
15. Che cosa è un centralino telefonico?
16. Se Lei vuol fare una telefonata e non sa il numero, che cosa può fare?
17. Chi conosce Lei che accetterebbe le spese se gli facesse una telefonata interurbana?
18. Quando si sente il segnale acustico?
19. Quando costa di meno una telefonata da stazione a stazione interurbana?
20. Quanti minuti corrispondono alla tariffa minima di una telefonata interurbana?

Temi per conversazione

1. Mio padre e il conto del telefono.
2. Come fare una telefonata interurbana con addebito al numero chiamato.
3. Una conversazione telefonica.

to listen (to) **ascoltare**	ski **lo sci**	guitar **la chitarra**
to play (*a musical instrument*) **suonare**	poster **il cartellone**	blanket **la coperta**
	key **la chiave**	bed **il letto**
to study **studiare**	key ring **il portachiavi**	bookcase **gli scaffali, la libreria**
to ski **sciare, fare lo sci**	cigarette **la sigaretta**	desk **la scrivania**
to smoke **fumare**	cigarette butt **la cicca**	notebook **il quaderno**
	package (*of cigarettes*) **il pacchetto**	pencil **la matita, il lapis**
room **la stanza, la camera**		wristwatch **l'orologio da polso**
roommate **il compagno (la compagna) di camera**	(cigarette) lighter **l'accendisigaro, l'accendino**	winter **l'inverno**
		snow **la neve**
dormitory **la residenza studentesca, la casa dello studente**	ashtray **il portacenere**	male **il maschio, il giovane**
	radio **la radio**	
wall **la parete**	lamp **la lampada**	at the same time **allo stesso tempo, al medesimo tempo**
window **la finestra**	light **la luce**	
windowsill **il davanzale**	bottle **la bottiglia**	

I compagni di camera

Analisi del disegno

1. Quale dei due compagni di camera sta studiando?
2. Quale dei due compagni di camera sta suonando la chitarra?
3. Che cosa c'è sulla scrivania?
4. Che c'è sul davanzale?
5. Che c'è accanto al davanzale?
6. Chi ha una matita e dov'è?
7. Come sa Lei che è di notte e non di giorno?
8. Dove stanno i cartelloni? Li descriva.
9. Dove sono le mani e le braccia dei ragazzi?
10. Chi porta un orologio da polso e dov'è?
11. Come sa Lei che qualcuno aveva fumato?
12. Alcuni libri sono sulla scrivania. Dove si trovano altri libri?

Punti di partenza

13. Crede Lei che questo disegno sia tipico di una stanza per maschi? Perchè?
14. Può Lei ascoltare la radio e studiare allo stesso tempo? Perchè?
15. Quanto costa un pacchetto di sigarette?
16. Preferisce Lei studiare di giorno o di notte? Perchè?
17. Che c'è sulla scrivania della Sua stanza?
18. Ha Lei dei cartelloni alla parete della Sua stanza? Li descriva. Se non li ha, perchè no?
19. Si può sciare vicino a dove vive Lei? Quando? Se non si può, perchè no?
20. Descriva una persona che Lei conosce che sappia suonare la chitarra.

Temi per conversazione

1. Vita di residenza studentesca.
2. Come (o come non) studiare.
3. La mia stanza all'università.

to mark the hem **segnare l'orlo**
to measure **misurare**
to put up one's hair **mettersi i bigodini**
to dry **asciugare**
to take time **prendere tempo**
to need **avere bisogno di**
to kneel **inginocchiarsi**

roommate **la compagna di camera**
girl **la ragazza, la signorina**
life (*with somebody*) **la convivenza, il convivere**
measure **la misura**
yard **la iarda**
yardstick **l'asta da una iarda**
meter **il metro**
centimeter **il centimetro**

inch **il pollice**
foot **il piede**
phonograph **il giradischi**
phonograph record **il disco**
coat hanger **l'attaccapanni**
photograph **la fotografia**
desk **la scrivania**
envelope **la busta**
stationery **la carta da scrivere**
letter **la lettera**
hair **i capelli**
curler (*for the hair*) **il bigodino**
pin **lo spillo**
pin box **la scatola per spilli**
bulletin board **il tabellone per affissi**
doll **la bambola**
mirror **lo specchio**
door **la porta**

sofa, couch **il sofà, il divano**
dress **il vestito**
stockings **le calze**
panty hose **il collant**
shoe **la scarpa**
sandal **il sandalo**
slacks (*for men or women*) **i calzoni, i pantaloni**
curtain **la tendina**
lamp **la lampada**
window **la finestra**
floor **il pavimento**
mouth **la bocca**
room (*space*) **lo spazio**
room (*habitation*) **la stanza, la camera**

useful **utile**

Le compagne di camera

Analisi del disegno

1. Come sa Lei che una delle ragazze ha scritto (o scriverà) una lettera?
2. Che oggetti ci sono sulla scrivania?
3. Dov'è l'attaccapanni e perchè sta lì?
4. Che sta facendo la ragazza con gli spilli in bocca?
5. Chi sta portando calzoni? Perchè?
6. Quale delle ragazze porta sandali? Perchè non li porta l'altra?
7. Che sta facendo la ragazza che si sta facendo segnare l'orlo?
8. Quante fotografie vede Lei e dove sono?
9. Che oggetti si vedono fra la porta e la lampada?
10. Perchè si è messa la sedia sotto la scrivania?
11. Perchè è la scatola per spilli dove sta?
12. Perchè si sta usando l'asta da una iarda?

Punti di partenza

13. Perchè è utile un tabellone per affissi?
14. Crede Lei che questo disegno sia tipico di una stanza per ragazze? Perchè?
15. Quanto tempo prende Lei per asciugare i suoi capelli?
16. Di quanti spilli ha bisogno Lei (più o meno) per segnare l'orlo di un vestito? Uno spillo per quanti centimetri o pollici?
17. Quando scrive lettere Lei e a chi?
18. Quanti pollici ci sono in un piede e quanti in una iarda?
19. Qual è la Sua misura in piedi e pollici?
20. Qual è la Sua misura in metri e centimetri? (1 metro = 3.28 piedi; 1 centimetro = .39 di pollice)

Temi per conversazione

1. La mia stanza all'università (o nella mia casa).
2. Come segnare un orlo.
3. Il convivere con il mio compagno (la mia compagna) di camera.

to lecture **fare una conferenza**
to take notes **prendere note,
  prendere appunti**
to teach **insegnare**
to study **studiare**
to pass **superare**
to fail **essere bocciato(a)**

student **lo studente, la studentessa**
professor **il professore, la professoressa**
college, university **l'università**
high school **la scuola second-
  aria, il collegio, il liceo**
course **il corso**

class **la classe**
classroom **l'aula**
lecture **la conferenza**
lecture hall **la sala da conferenze**
blackboard **la lavagna**
chalk **il gesso**
bench **il banco**
level **il livello**
building **l'edificio**
model, mock-up **il modello**
skull **il cranio**
bridge **il ponte**
glasses **gli occhiali**
table **la tavola**
writer **lo scrittore**

face **la faccia (le facce,** *pl.***), il
  viso**
anatomy **l'anatomia**
architecture **l'architettura**
engineering **l'ingegneria**
literature **la letteratura**

right-handed **che usa la mano
  destra**
left-handed **mancino, che usa la
  mano sinistra**
with his (her) back to **con le
  spalle a**
same **stesso**

La sala da conferenze

Analisi del disegno

1. Chi porta occhiali in questi disegni?
2. Come sa Lei qual è la classe di anatomia?
3. Che cosa sta facendo il professore nella classe sopra la cui tavola si vede il modello di un edificio?
4. Chi sta dimostrando un modello di un ponte?
5. Che cosa sta insegnando la professoressa?
6. In quali due classi non si vedono le facce degli studenti?
7. Perchè non possiamo vedere la faccia del professore di architettura?
8. Qual è la differenza tra i banchi della classe di anatomia e quei della classe d'ingegneria?
9. In che classe si vede il numero minore di studenti?
10. Quale delle quattro classi Le interesserebbe di più? Perchè?
11. Quali usano la mano destra e quali la mano sinistra in questi disegni?

Punti di partenza

12. Chi era Shakespeare?
13. Che è ciò che Le piace di più nell'essere studente?
14. Che è ciò che Le piace di meno nell'essere studente?
15. Con che si scrive sulla lavagna?
16. Quando si prendono note?
17. Qual è la differenza tra un'aula ed una sala da conferenze?
18. Le piacerebbe essere professore? Perchè? Se no, perchè no?
19. Quali sono alcune differenze tra un liceo ed un'università?
20. Quanti corsi ha Lei adesso e quali sono due di essi?

Temi per conversazione

1. La ragione per la quale non voglio essere bocciato (-a) a questo corso.
2. Come superare senza studiare.
3. La descrizione della mia classe d'italiano.

to read **leggere**
to write **scrivere**
to browse, to leaf through **sfogliare**
to lend **prestare**
to study **studiare**
to leave, to go out **andarsene**

library **la biblioteca**
librarian **il bibliotecario, la bibliotecaria**
professor **il professore, la professoressa**
student **lo studente, la studentessa**
book **il libro**
magazine **la rivista**
briefcase **la cartella**
dictionary **il dizionario**
word **la parola**
definition **la definizione**

encyclopedia **l'enciclopedia**
atlas **l'atlante geografico**
information **l'informazione** (*f.*)
reference book **il libro di consultazione**
play **il dramma, il lavoro teatrale**
poem **il poema, la poesia**
novel **il romanzo**
short story **il racconto, la novella**
plot **l'intreccio**
fiction **la narrativa, il romanzo, la novella, la poesia, il dramma**
nonfiction **la letteratura nonnarrativa, la biografia, la storia, l'opera scientifica**
bookshelf **lo scaffale**
bookshelves, shelving **la libreria, gli scaffali**
glasses **gli occhiali**

skirt **la gonna**
sweater **il maglione, il pullover**
chair **la sedia**
arm **il braccio (le braccia,** *pl.***)**
hand **la mano (le mani,** *pl.***)**
hair **i capelli**
room **la stanza**
majority **la maggioranza, la maggior parte**

yesterday **ieri**
almost **quasi**
long **lungo**
short **corto**
lately **ultimamente**
quiet **silenzioso**
imaginary **immaginario**
true **vero, verace**
noisy **rumoroso**
quiet **quieto**

La biblioteca

___

Analisi del disegno

1. Quante persone si possono vedere in questo disegno?
2. Che sta facendo la maggioranza degli studenti?
3. Chi se ne va e che tiene nella mano?
4. Chi ha i capelli lunghi? I capelli corti? Chi è quasi senza capelli?
5. Dov'è la maggior parte dei libri?
6. Come sa Lei che questa è una biblioteca?
7. Descriva la studentessa in primo piano.
8. Che sta facendo la ragazza davanti agli scaffali per riviste?

Punti di partenza

9. Che è una biblioteca?
10. Ci spieghi la differenza tra « scaffale » e « libreria ».
11. Generalmente, qual è la differenza nella maniera di portare i libri di un ragazzo e di una ragazza?
12. Dove studia meglio Lei, nella biblioteca o nella Sua stanza? Perchè?
13. Che è un libro di consultazione? Nomini due libri di consultazione.
14. Spieghi la differenza tra un dizionario e un'enciclopedia.
15. Spieghi la differenza tra la letteratura narrativa e la letteratura non-narrativa.
16. Descriva l'intreccio di un racconto o di un romanzo che Lei ha letto.
17. Che è « sfogliare » ?
18. Perchè non si deve scrivere nei libri della biblioteca?
19. Quali sono alcune differenze fra un libro ed una rivista?
20. Descriva la biblioteca della Sua università.

Temi per conversazione

1. Andandomene dalla biblioteca ieri . . . .
2. Un buon libro che ho letto ultimamente.
3. Ciò che si trova in una biblioteca.

to dance **ballare**
to check one's coat **depositare il cappotto**
to sing **cantare**
to stay out late **rimaner fuori tardi**
to have fun (to enjoy oneself) **divertirsi**
to play (*music, a musical instrument, or a phonograph record*) **suonare**
to smile **sorridere**
to laugh **ridere**
to hire **prendere in affitto, noleggiare**
to resemble **somigliarsi**

dance **il ballo**
cloakroom **il (la) guardaroba**

phonograph **il giradischi, il grammofono**
phonograph record **il disco**
intermission **la pausa, l'intervallo**
refreshment **il rinfresco, il rinfrescante**
pitcher **la brocca**
glass **il bicchiere**
tray **il vassoio**
sandwich **il panino imbottito, il sandwich**
bracelet **il braccialetto**
musician **il musicista, il sonatore**
guitar **la chitarra**
drum **il tamburo**
wind instrument **lo strumento a fiato**

trumpet **la trombetta, la tromba**
trombone **il trombone**
clarinet **il clarinetto**
saxophone **il sassofono**
waltz **il valzer**
rock music **il «rock»**
folk music **la musica popolare, la musica folcloristica**
teenager, adolescent **il teenager, l'adolescente** (*m. & f.*)
partner (*at a dance*) **il compagno (la compagna) di ballo, il cavaliere, la dama**
wall **la parete**
mouth **la bocca**

happy **felice**
different **diverso**
obvious, evident **ovvio**

Il ballo

Analisi del disegno

1. Che sono e dove stanno i rinfrescanti?
2. Chi pare essere la persona più felice di questo disegno e perchè?
3. Che cosa è un(a) guardaroba e dove si trova in questo disegno?
4. Quali delle signorine del disegno portano braccialetti?
5. Dia una descrizione dei musicisti.
6. Perchè è ovvio che i giovani del disegno si stanno divertendo?
7. Dove sono le decorazioni?
8. Che tipo di musica pare star suonando l'orchestra?
9. Chi non stanno ballando?
10. Descriva il disegno.

Punti di partenza

11. Quando va a un ballo con un compagno che non conosce molto bene, di che cosa possono parlare?
12. Qual è una delle differenze tra il valzer ed il « rock »?
13. In che si somigliano una trombetta, un clarinetto, un sassofono ed un trombone?
14. Che è l'ora più tarda che Lei è rimasto fuori di notte? Quando? Per quale occasione?
15. Quale strumento musicale è più tipico per la musica folcloristica?
16. Per quanto tempo è uno un teen-ager?
17. Qual è la differenza fra musica classica e musica semiclassica?
18. Dove si deposita il cappotto durante un ballo?
19. Come possono dare un ballo i giovani senza prendere in affitto un'orchestra?
20. Che cosa si può fare durante le pause dell'orchestra?

Temi per conversazione

1. Diversi tipi di musica.
2. Quello che succede quando rimango fuori troppo tardi di notte.
3. Descrizione di un ballo all'università.

to breathe **respirare**	neck **il collo**	toenail **l'unghia del dito del**
to bend **piegare**	shoulder **la spalla**	**piede**
to weigh **pesare**	back **la schiena, il dorso**	bone **l'osso (le ossa,** *pl.***)**
to stay, to remain **rimaner(si)**	chest, breast **il petto**	joint **l'articolazione (** *f.* **)**
to join, to connect **unire**	arm **il braccio (le braccia,** *pl.***)**	skin **la pelle**
to close **chiudere**	elbow **il gomito**	blood **il sangue**
	wrist **il polso**	artery **l'arteria**
body **il corpo**	hand **la mano (le mani,** *pl.***)**	vein **la vena**
face **la faccia (le facce,** *pl.***) il**	palm **la palma**	heart **il cuore**
viso	knuckle **la nocca**	stomach **lo stomaco**
head **la testa, il capo**	finger **il dito (le dita,** *pl.***)**	lung **il pulmone**
forehead, brow **la fronte**	thumb **il pollice**	muscle **il muscolo**
skull **il cranio**	index finger **l'indice (** *m.* **)**	male **il maschio**
brain **il cervello**	middle finger **il medio**	female **la femmina**
hair **i capelli**	ring finger **l'anulare (** *m.* **)**	
eye **l'occhio**	little finger **il mignolo**	
eyelid **la palpebra**	ring **l'anello**	healthy **sano**
eyelash **la ciglia**	fingernail **l'unghia**	unhealthy **malsano**
eyebrow **il sopracciglio**	fist **il pugno**	strong **forte**
ear **l'orecchio**	waist **la vita, la cintura**	weak **debole**
nose **il naso**	hip **l'anca**	tall **grande, alto**
cheek **la guancia**	buttock **la natica**	short **piccolo, basso**
temple **la tempia**	thigh **la coscia**	slender, thin **snello, esile**
jaw **la mascella, la mandibola**	leg **la gamba**	fat, heavy **grasso, pesante**
mouth **la bocca**	knee **il ginocchio**	young, **giovane**
lip **il labbro (le labbra,** *pl.***)**	calf **il polpaccio**	old **vecchio**
tongue **la lingua**	ankle **la caviglia**	married **sposato**
tooth **il dente**	foot **il piede**	single **celibe**
chin **il mento**	toe **il dito del piede**	right **destro**
		left **sinistro**

14

Il corpo umano

Analisi del disegno

1. Descriva l'aspetto fisico generale del maschio.
2. Perchè (non) Le pare sana la femmina del disegno?
3. Chi è più alto? Chi pesa più?

Punti di partenza

4. Che unisce la testa alle spalle?
5. Nomini le parti della faccia.
6. Spieghi le differenze tra sporacciglio e ciglia.
7. Che c'è dentro il cranio?
8. Quanti denti ha la maggioranza degli adulti?
9. Se una persona è grassa, in quale parte del corpo è questa condizione ordinariamente più evidente?
10. Che trasporta il sangue al cuore e dal cuore?
11. Quante dita del piede abbiamo?
12. Che sono i nomi delle dita in italiano?
13. Se Lei porta un anello, su quale dito di quale mano lo porta? Se non porta un anello, perchè no?
14. Nomini una parte esteriore del corpo sulla quale non c'è pelle.
15. Che succede nei polmoni?
16. Nomini tutte le parti del corpo sotto la coscia.
17. Nocca, polso, gomito, ginocchio—qual è la somiglianza fra loro?
18. Dov'è la palma della mano?
19. Come si chiama la mano chiusa?
20. Nomini due parti del corpo visibili solamente da dietro e due non visibili da dietro.

Temi per conversazione

1. Come funziona il corpo umano.
2. La circolazione del sangue.
3. Come rimanere giovane.

1976

	Gennaio	Febbraio	Marzo	Aprile

```
        D L M M G V S        D L M M G V S        D L M M G V S        D L M M G V S
             Gennaio              Febbraio              Marzo                Aprile
                  1 2 3     1 2 3 4 5 6 7        1 2 3 4 5 6              1 2 3
    4 5 6 7 8 9 10      8 9 10 11 12 13 14    7 8 9 10 11 12 13    4 5 6 7 8 9 10
   11 12 13 14 15 16 17  15 16 17 18 19 20 21   14 15 16 17 18 19 20   11 12 13 14 15 16 17
   18 19 20 21 22 23 24  22 23 24 25 26 27 28   21 22 23 24 25 26 27   18 19 20 21 22 23 24
   25 26 27 28 29 30 31  29                     28 29 30 31           25 26 27 28 29 30

            Maggio               Giugno                Luglio               Agosto
                      1       1 2 3 4 5              1 2 3      1 2 3 4 5 6 7
    2 3 4 5 6 7 8       6 7 8 9 10 11 12     4 5 6 7 8 9 10     8 9 10 11 12 13 14
    9 10 11 12 13 14 15   13 14 15 16 17 18 19   11 12 13 14 15 16 17   15 16 17 18 19 20 21
   16 17 18 19 20 21 22   20 21 22 23 24 25 26   18 19 20 21 22 23 24   22 23 24 25 26 27 28
   23 24 25 26 27 28 29   27 28 29 30           25 26 27 28 29 30 31   29 30 31
   30 31

           Settembre             Ottobre              Novembre             Dicembre
             1 2 3 4                 1 2       1 2 3 4 5 6          1 2 3 4
    5 6 7 8 9 10 11     3 4 5 6 7 8 9      7 8 9 10 11 12 13    5 6 7 8 9 10 11
   12 13 14 15 16 17 18   10 11 12 13 14 15 16   14 15 16 17 18 19 20   12 13 14 15 16 17 18
   19 20 21 22 23 24 25   17 18 19 20 21 22 23   21 22 23 24 25 26 27   19 20 21 22 23 24 25
   26 27 28 29 30        24 25 26 27 28 29 30   28 29 30             26 27 28 29 30 31
                          31
```

to fall, to occur **cadere**
to celebrate **celebrare, festeggiare**
to be implied **essere implicito**
to take place **aver luogo**

calendar **il calendario**
date **la data**
month **il mese**
week **la settimana**
Sunday **la domenica**
Monday **il lunedì**
Tuesday **il martedì**
Wednesday **il mercoledì**
Thursday **il giovedì**
Friday **il venerdì**
Saturday **il sabato**
year **l'anno**
leap year **l'anno bisestile**
school year **l'anno scolastico**
hour, time **l'ora**

minute **il minuto**
second **il secondo**
noon **il mezzogiorno**
midnight **la mezzanotte**
standard time **l'ora ufficiale**
daylight saving time **l'ora estiva**
daylight **la luce del giorno**
vernal equinox **l'equinozio di primavera**
autumnal equinox **l'equinozio di autunno**
spring **la primavera**
summer **l'estate** (*f.*)
fall **l'autunno**
winter **l'inverno**
workday **il giorno feriale, il giorno lavorativo**
holiday **la festa, il giorno festivo**
weekend **il (la) fine settimana, il weekend**
long weekend **il ponte (di fine settimana)**
birthday **il compleanno**
saint's day **il giorno della festa del santo**
Christmas **il Natale**
Easter **la Pasqua**
New Year's Day **il capodanno**
eve **la vigilia**
Independence Day (U.S.A.) **la festa dell'indipendenza**
Labor Day (U.S.A.) **la festa del lavoro**
Memorial Day (U.S.A.) **il giorno (della commemorazione) dei caduti**
country **il paese**
horoscope **l'oroscopo**
life **la storia**

long **lungo**
short **corto**

Il calendario

Analisi del disegno

1. Quali giorni della settimana son generalmente giorni lavorativi?
2. Quali mesi hanno trentun giorni? Quali ne hanno trenta?
3. Che cosa è implicita nell'espressione « fine settimana »? E nell'espressione « un ponte di fine settimana »?
4. In quale giorno della settimana cade il Natale nell'anno 1976? Ed il giorno di 200 anni dell'indipendenza degli Stati Uniti?
5. In che data cade la festa del lavoro nell'anno 1976? Il giorno dei caduti? La vigilia del capodanno?
6. In che mesi del calendario dell'anno 1976 cade un venerdì con la data 13?
7. Quali mesi dell'anno 1976 hanno il maggior numero di domeniche?
8. Quanti giorni ha la settimana? Quante settimane ha l'anno? Quanti giorni ha l'anno? Quanti mesi ha l'anno?

Punti di partenza

9. Quanti secondi ci sono in un minuto? Quanti minuti in un'ora? Quante ore in un giorno?
10. L'anno 1976 è bisestile. Quanti anni bisestili ci sono stati durante la Sua vita?
11. Quando è il Suo compleanno?
12. Nomini un giorno festivo in Italia che non si festeggia negli Stati Uniti.
13. Che cosa è « equinozio »? In quali mesi hanno luogo gli equinozi di primavera e di autunno?
14. Quali mesi hanno i giorni più lunghi e quali i più corti?
15. Quante ore ci sono tra il mezzogiorno e la mezzanotte?
16. Qual è lo svantaggio dell'ora ufficiale durante l'estate?
17. Nomini tre anni importanti della storia degli Stati Uniti e spieghi perchè sono importanti.
18. La festa del giorno del santo si celebra nei paesi cattolici. Spieghì che cos'è.
19. Quali sono più o meno i mesi d'inverno, di primavera, d'estate e d'autunno?
20. Il compleanno di chi è festa nazionale negli Stati Uniti, e in che data ha luogo?

Temi per conversazione

1. Come si sa quando cade il giorno di Pasqua.
2. Le feste più importanti dell'anno scolastico.
3. Il mio oroscopo.

to sleep **dormire**
to fall asleep **addormentarsi**
to watch TV **guardare la televisione**
to knit **fare la maglia, lavorare a
maglia**

member of the family **il mem-
bro della famiglia**
husband **il marito**
wife **la moglie**
son **il figlio**
daughter **la figlia**
nephew **il nipote**
niece **la nipote**
grandfather **il nonno**
grandmother **la nonna**

brother **il fratello**
sister **la sorella**
uncle **lo zio**
aunt **la zia**
cousin **il cugino, la cugina**
relationship (*family*) **la parentela**
home **il focolare**
living room **il salotto**
window **la finestra**
television set **il televisore**
television **la televisione**
color television **la televisione a
colori**
channel **il canale**
station **la stazione**
commercial **l'annuncio pubbli-**

citario, **la pubblicità**
transistor radio **il transistore**
furniture **la mobilia, i mobili**
armchair **la poltrona**
sofa, couch **il sofà, il divano**
table **la tavola**
lamp **la lampada**
magazine **la rivista**
lap **il grembo**
glasses **gli occhiali**
slipper **la pantofola**
evening **la serata, la sera**

comfortable **comodo**
at home **in casa, a casa**
while **mentre**

La famiglia

Analisi del disegno

1. Che ora della sera crede Lei che sia? Perchè?
2. Chi stanno seduti sul divano?
3. Dov'è il televisore?
4. Che sta facendo la madre mentre guarda la televisione?
5. Descriva i mobili.
6. Che sta facendo il ragazzino?
7. Crede Lei che il padre sia comodo? Che sta facendo?
8. Com'è vestito il padre?
9. Come sa Lei che il padre stava leggendo?
10. Chi pare più giovane, il ragazzino o la ragazzina? Perchè?

Punti di partenza

11. Che cosa Le piace fare di più quando Lei è a casa per la serata?
12. Qual è il Suo programma di televisione preferito e perchè è il Suo preferito?
13. Alla radio e alla televisione, che è un annuncio pubblicitario?
14. Qual è la differenza tra « canale » e « stazione »?
15. Quanto piccolo può essere un transistore?
16. Qual è la differenza tra « casa » e « focolare »?
17. Che è la Sua parentela con la sorella di Suo padre? Con la figlia di suo nonno? Con la figlia del fratello di Sua madre? Con Suo zio?
18. Descriva il marito o la moglie che ha Lei o che spera di avere un giorno.
19. Descriva quella che è, nella Sua opinione, una famiglia ideale; ciò vuol dire, quanti membri e perchè?
20. Dove e quando guarda Lei la televisione?

Temi per conversazione

1. Perchè generalmente la televisione (non) mi piace.
2. Perchè il padre si è addormentato.
3. Il mio focolare e la mia famiglia.

to own **essere proprietario di, possedere**	furnace, heating plant **il calorifero**	lamp **la lampada**
to rent **affittare**	garbage can **il bidone dei rifiuti, il porta-immondizie**	bureau, chest of drawers **il cassettone**
to make the bed **fare il letto**		desk **la scrivania**
to clean house **pulire la casa**	curtain, drape **la tendina, il panneggio**	chair **la sedia**
to dust **spolverare**		armchair **la poltrona**
to scrub **strofinare**	window **la finestra**	footstool, hassock **lo sgabello per i piedi**
to play (*a musical instrument*) **suonare**	doorway **la porta, l'ingresso**	
	wall **la parete**	trunk **il baule**
	room **la stanza, la camera**	floor (*on which one walks*) **il pavimento**
home, hearth **il focolare**	living room **il salotto**	
two-story house **la casa a due piani**	dining room **la sala da pranzo**	floor (*story*) **il piano**
	bedroom **la camera da letto**	apartment **l'appartamento**
groundfloor **il pianterreno**	bathroom **la stanza da bagno, il bagno**	"dream house" **la casa dei sogni**
upper floor **il piano superiore**		mortgage **l'ipoteca**
cellar, basement **la cantina**	kitchen **la cucina**	maid **la cameriera**
attic **la soffitta**	corridor **il corridoio**	(domestic) duties **i lavori (domestici)**
roof **il tetto**	furniture **la mobilia, i mobili**	
stairway **la scala**	dining-room table **la tavola da pranzo**	
chimney **il camino**		instead of **invece di**
fireplace **il caminetto**	planter **la giardiniera**	what else? **che cos'altro?**
lightning rod **il parafulmine**	rug **il tappeto**	

Il focolare

Analisi del disegno

1. Quante stanze ha questa casa e quali sono?
2. Dove sono i bidoni dei rifiuti?
3. Che vede Lei nella soffitta?
4. Dove vede Lei un tappeto in questa casa?
5. Perchè ha un caminetto questa casa?
6. Che cos'altro c'è sul tetto?
7. Descriva ciò che vede nella sala da pranzo.
8. Dov'è la cucina?
9. Le piacerebbe di abitare in questa casa? Perchè? Perchè no?
10. Quale poltrona ha uno sgabello per i piedi?
11. Dov'è il bagno che si può vedere?
12. Dov'è la scala?
13. Perchè può vedere il ragazzo suonare il pianoforte di giorno o di notte?
14. Perchè crede Lei che sia di giorno, o perchè crede che sia di notte?

Punti di partenza

15. Quali sono i lavori di una cameriera?
16. Descriva una soffitta tipica.
17. Perchè c'è molta gente che preferisce affittare appartamenti invece di essere proprietaria di casa?
18. Perchè c'è molta gente che preferisce essere proprietaria invece di affittare appartamenti?
19. Che ha generalmente la gente nei bauli nella soffitta?
20. Spieghi che cos'è un'ipoteca.

Temi per conversazione

1. La casa dei miei sogni.
2. Le stanze ed i mobili di una casa.
3. Come pulire una casa.

to be hungry **avere fame**	oven **il forno**	oil **l'olio**
to cook **cucinare**	sink **l'acquaio, il lavandino**	bottle **la bottiglia**
to take (*to eat, drink*) **prendere**	fan **il ventilatore**	casserole **la casseruola**
to serve **servire**	refrigerator **il frigorifero**	ladle **il mestolo**
to wash dishes **lavare i piatti**	handle **la maniglia**	glass **il bicchiere**
to scold **rimproverare**	closet **l'armadio**	wine **il vino**
to place **collocare, mettere**	coffee **il caffè**	cork **il tappo**
to take out, to remove **togliere**	coffee pot **la caffettiera**	plate **il piatto**
to open **aprire**	cup **la tazza**	napkin **il tovagliolo**
	apron **il grembiale, il grembiule**	meal **il pasto**
kitchen **la cucina**	basket (*for bread*) **il cestino**	food **il cibo, l'alimento**
stove, kitchen range **la cucina (a**	**(per il pane)**	detergent **il detersivo**
gas)	roll **il panino**	windowsill **il davanzale**
burner **il fornello**	salad **l'insalata**	flower pot **il vaso da fiori**
back burner **il fornello poste-**	salad bowl **l'insalatiera**	
riore	salt **il sale**	each (one) **ciascuno**
front burner **il fornello ante-**	pepper **il pepe**	still, yet **ancora**
riore	vinegar **l'aceto**	

La cucina

Analisi del disegno

1. Chi crede Lei che abbia più fame? Perchè?
2. Chi sta rimproverando chi?
3. Che cosa tiene il padre nella mano e che sta facendo?
4. Che sta facendo la madre?
5. Su quale fornello si trova la caffettiera?
6. Quando si servirà il caffè? Come lo sa Lei?
7. Che oggetti ci sono sul davanzale dietro il frigorifero?
8. Crede Lei che il frigorifero sia ben collocato? Perchè? Perchè no?
9. Perchè è mal collocata la maniglia della porta del frigorifero?
10. Dove c'è un armadio? Un ventilatore?
11. Quali prenderanno il vino e perchè lo sa?
12. Ci sono quattro bottiglie in questo disegno. Che contiene ciascuna?
13. Quando mangeranno la frutta?
14. Descriva i ragazzini.
15. Perchè ci sono più piatti che gente?
16. Come sa che la bottiglia di vino è già stata aperta e che nessuno se n'è ancora servito?
17. Dove vede il sale ed il pepe?

Punti di partenza

18. Perchè si mette un tovagliolo sopra il pane o i panini dentro il cestino quando si tolgono dal forno?
19. Quando si porta un grembiale?
20. Preferisce Lei lavare i piatti o cucinare? Perchè?

Temi per conversazione

1. Questa scena può essere europea o americana.
2. Vantaggi e svantaggi di mangiare in cucina.
3. Il pasto e come si serve nella mia università.

to turn **girare**
to turn on (to run) the water **far scorrere l'acqua**
to turn off the water **chiudere l'acqua**
to take a bath **bagnarsi, farsi un bagno**
to take a shower **(far(si) una doccia**
to wash (up) **lavarsi**
to dry (off) **asciugarsi**
to splash **schizzare, spruzzare**
to brush one's teeth **spazzolarsi i denti**
to shave (oneself) **radersi, farsi la barba**

bathroom **la stanza da bagno, il bagno**
bathrobe **l'accappatoio**
towel **l'asciugamano**
towel rack **il portasciugamano**
sink **il lavabo**

faucet, spigot **il rubinetto**
soap **il sapone**
toothbrush **lo spazzolino da denti**
toothpaste **il dentifricio**
electric razor **il rasoio elettrico**
safety razor **il rasoio di sicurezza**
straight razor, barber's razor **il rasoio**
shaving cream **la crema da barba**
cord **il cordone**
(electrical) plug **la spina di corrente**
(electric) outlet **la presa di corrente**
(electrical) shock **la scossa (elettrica)**
bottle **la bottiglia**
nail polish **lo smalto per le unghie**

mirror **lo specchio**
glass (*container*) **il bicchiere**
ceiling **il soffitto**
floor **il pavimento**
toilet **il gabinetto, il water closet**
bidet **il bidè (bidet)**
bathtub **la vasca da bagno**
shower **la doccia**
(shower) curtain **la tendina (di doccia)**
shelf **la mensola**
pajamas **il pigiama**
rug **il tappeto**
fan **il ventilatore**
counter **il banco**

alone **solo**
how often? **con che frequenza?**
as well as **tanto ... come**

24

Il bagno

Analisi del disegno

1. Come sa Lei che l'uomo va a farsi un bagno e non una doccia?
2. Perchè può essere questo bagno tanto europeo come americano?
3. Che c'è sul pavimento?
4. In che tre luoghi ci sono asciugamani?
5. Dov'è la presa di corrente per il rasoio elettrico?
6. Dove c'è un ventilatore?
7. Quali oggetti si possono vedere davanti all'uomo e alla sua destra?
8. Dov'è il water closet? Dov'è il bidè (bidet)?
9. Che porta l'uomo?
10. Che c'è ad ogni estremità del cordone?
11. Quali oggetti del disegno Le fanno supporre che quest'uomo non viva solo?
12. Perchè non vede Lei crema da barba in questo disegno?
13. Perchè non dovrebbe essere la presa di corrente tanto vicino al lavabo come si trova qui?

Punti di partenza

14. Per che cosa si usano gli asciugamani?
15. Per che cosa si usa una tendina di doccia?
16. Come si fa scorrere o si chiude l'acqua?
17. Si fa una doccia prima di farsi la barba o dopo? Perchè?
18. Con che frequenza si spazzola Lei i denti?
19. Spieghi la differenza tra la funzione di una vasca da bagno e la funzione di un lavabo.
20. Preferisce la doccia o il bagno? Perchè?

Temi per conversazione

1. Le stanze da bagno—antiche e moderne.
2. I vantaggi di un rasoio elettrico.
3. Dell'uomo che mise crema da barba sul suo spazzolino da denti.

to set the table **apparecchiare la tavola**
to clear the table **sparecchiare la tavola**
to serve **servire**
to pour **versare**
to make a toast **fare un brindisi**
to place **mettere, porre**
to sit down **sedersi**

etiquette **l'etichetta**
usage **l'usanza**
host **l'ospite** (*m. & f.*)
guest **l'invitato, il convitato**
tablecloth **la tovaglia**
napkin **il tovagliolo**
place setting (*utensils collectively*) **il coperto, la posata**
soup bowl **la scodella**
saucer **il piattino**
service plate **il piatto piano**
butter plate **il piattino per il burro**

dinner knife **il coltello**
butter knife **il coltello per il burro**
dinner fork **la forchetta**
salad fork **la forchetta per l'insalata**
dessert fork **la forchetta per il dolce**
teaspoon **il cucchiaino da tè**
soup spoon, tablespoon **il cucchiaio da tavola**
pitcher **la brocca**
water **l'acqua**
wine **il vino**
wine basket **il portafiaschi**
handle (*of a basket or pitcher*) **il manico**
waterglass **il bicchiere da acqua**
wine glass **il bicchiere da vino**
saltshaker **la saliera**
pepper shaker **la pepaiola**
ashtray **il portacenere**
cigarette **la sigaretta**

(cigarette) lighter **l'accendisigaro, l'accendino**
chair **la sedia**
flower arrangement, centerpiece **il centro tavola (di fiori)**
head of the table **il capotavola**
center of the table **il centro della tavola**
main meal, dinner **il pranzo**
dinner (*supper*) **la cena**
waiter **il cameriere**
waitress **la cameriera**
tray **il vassoio**
place **il posto**

formal **formale, d'etichetta**
informal **informale, senza ceremonie**
according to form (*formal or informal*) **formale**
still, yet **ancora**

26

La tavola

Analisi del disegno

1. Come sa Lei che il pranzo non è stato ancora servito?
2. Come sa Lei che questo pranzo sarà d'etichetta?
3. Che cosa si servirà nei due bicchieri?
4. È la forchetta a sinistra una forchetta per l'insalata o una forchetta per il dolce? Perchè?
5. C'è qualcosa che Le indica che la tavola non è stata apparecchiata secondo l'usanza americana? Se è così, lo spieghi.
6. Perchè ci sono un cucchiaio da tavola e un cucchiaino da tè ad ogni coperto?
7. Dove son stati messi i tovaglioli?
8. Che c'è al centro della tavola?
9. Chi si sederà a capotavola?
10. Se ci sono due ospiti, quanti invitati verranno al pranzo?
11. Che c'è a destra di ogni piatto?
12. Dove sono la saliera e la pepaiola?
13. Dove son stati messi i coltelli per il burro?
14. Perchè stanno i portafiaschi nei posti dove sono?
15. Quali cose ci sono sui piccoli vassoi davanti agli ospiti?
16. Alla sinistra di chi starà la brocca?

Punti di partenza

17. Come si fa un brindisi?
18. Quali sono i compiti di un cameriere o di una cameriera?
19. Qual è la differenza tra un piatto e un piattino? Tra un cucchiaio e un cucchiaino da tè?
20. Che direbbe Lei a un invitato che Le dice che non gli è piaciuto il pranzo che Lei gli ha servito?

Temi per conversazione

1. L'etichetta per apparecchiare una tavola.
2. Come servire un pranzo d'etichetta.
3. I vini.

to play (*a sport*) **giocare (a)**	tennis player **il (la) tennista, il giocatore di tennis, la giocatrice di tennis**	singles **il singolo**
to win **vincere**		doubles **il doppio**
to lose **perdere**		spectator, fan **lo spettatore, il tifoso**
to hit (*a ball*) **battere**	sport **lo sport**	
to throw **lanciare**	game, match **il gioco, la partita**	(metal) screen **la rete metallica**
to serve (*a ball*) **servire**	court **il campo da tennis, il campo da gioco**	bench **la panca**
to harm, to hurt **danneggiarsi, far(si) male a**		stool **lo sgabello**
to warp **curvarsi**	net **la rete**	wall (*exterior*) **il muro**
to be accustomed to **avere l'abitudine**	ball **la palla da tennis**	rain **la pioggia**
	raquet **la racchetta**	sunglasses **gli occhiali da sole**
	press **la pressa per racchetta**	softdrink **la gassosa, la bibita**
tennis **il tennis**	serve **il servizio**	
	point **il punto**	high **alto**
		low **basso**

Il tennis

Analisi del disegno

1. Chi portano occhiali da sole?
2. È un singolo o un doppio questa partita?
3. Quanti spettatori ci sono? Dove stanno?
4. Crede Lei che le due persone in primo piano non abbiano ancora giocato o che abbiano già giocato? Perchè?
5. Perchè c'è una rete metallica nel fondo del campo da gioco?
6. Chi stanno seduti è sopra che?
7. Dove c'è un muro?
8. Quante persone nel campo da gioco hanno l'abitudine di usare la mano destra, e come lo sa Lei?
9. Chi ha una gassosa ed in quale mano la tiene?
10. Come sa Lei che si sta giocando la partita di giorno e non di sera?

Punti di partenza

11. Il tennis è uno sport internazionale. Che cosa vuol dire questo?
12. Qual è il massimo ed il minimo numero di giocatori in una partita di tennis?
13. Quanto può costare una buona racchetta?
14. I giocatori di tennis hanno l'abitudine di tenere le loro racchette in una pressa quando non stanno sul campo da gioco. Perchè?
15. Alcuni giochi possono essere giocati sotto la pioggia. Perchè non il tennis?
16. Che è un tifoso?
17. Descriva le differenze fra una panca e uno sgabello.
18. Perchè può o non può Lei giocare a tennis oggi?
19. Quando in una partita di tennis batte Lei la palla prima del Suo avversario?
20. Di chi è il punto se Lei batte la palla contro la rete?

Temi per conversazione

1. Dialogo fra il ragazzo e la ragazza che stanno in primo piano di questo disegno.
2. Descrizione dei campi da tennis della mia università.
3. « Non dipende da se si vince o si perde, ma da come si è giocato ».

to have (go on) a picnic **fare un pic-nic, fare una scampagnata**
to make a sandwich **preparare un panino imbottito, fare un sandwich**
to cut, to slice **tagliare a fette**
to pack (to prepare) **impaccare, preparare**
to forget **dimenticare**
to park **parcheggiare, stazionare**
to kneel **inginocchiarsi**
to discard, to throw away **scartare, gettare via**
to tell, to narrate **raccontare**
to uncork **sturare, stappare**

picnic **il pic-nic, la scampagnata**

tree **l'albero**
grass **l'erba**
automobile, car **l'automobile (f.), la macchina**
food **il cibo**
loaf of bread **il pane**
piece (slice) of bread **la fetta di pane, il pezzo di pane**
sausage **la salsiccia**
cheese **il formaggio**
sandwich **il panino imbottito, il sandwich**
beverage **la bevanda**
wine **il vino**
softdrink **la gassosa, la bibita**
knife **il coltello**
picnic basket **il cestino**

bottle **la bottiglia**
cork **il tappo**
corkscrew **il cavatappi**
thermos jug **il thermos**
paper cup **la tazza di carta**
paper plate **il piatto di carta**
ant **la formica**
fly **la mosca**
mosquito **la zanzara**

sunny **soleggiato**
shady **ombroso, all'ombra, ombreggiato**
never, ever **mai**
...style **al modo...**
agreeable **gradevole**
disagreeable **sgradevole**

30

Una scampagnata

Analisi del disegno

1. Che cosa Le fa credere che questa sia una scena europea?
2. Dov'è stata parcheggiata la macchina?
3. Che sta facendo il ragazzo che sta inginocchiato?
4. Che sta facendo la ragazza?
5. Che sta facendo il ragazzo che tiene un coltello?
6. Quali altre cose possono avere nel cestino?
7. Descriva il luogo.
8. Ci racconti di che cosa possono parlare i giovani.
9. Che cosa tiene ogni persona nella sua mano sinistra?
10. Che cosa tiene ogni persona nella sua mano destra?
11. Le piacerebbe fare una scampagnata in un luogo come questo? Perchè? Perchè no?

Punti di partenza

12. Perchè è gradevole un pic-nic?
13. Quali sono gli aspetti sgradevoli di un pic-nic?
14. Preferisce Lei un luogo ombroso o soleggiato per un pic-nic? Perchè?
15. Come si prepara un panino imbottito?
16. Per che cosa serve un thermos?
17. Qual è il vantaggio di usare tazze e piatti di carta?
18. Che farebbe Lei durante una scampagnata se avesse dimenticato il cestino con il cibo e le bibite?
19. Che cosa farebbe Lei se trovasse formiche nel Suo panino imbottito?
20. Quali sono le cose che s'impaccano per una scampagnata al modo americano?

Temi per conversazione

1. Perchè mi piace (non mi piace) una scampagnata.
2. Come preparare un cestino per un pic-nic.
3. Una scampagnata che non dimenticherò mai.

to swim **nuotare**
to sunbathe **prendere il sole**
to get a sun tan **abbronzarsi**
to float **stare a galla, galleggiare**
to surf **fare il « surfing »**
to play **giocare**
to dig **scavare**
to warn **avvertire**
to tell, to relate **raccontare**
to avoid **evitare**
to try to **cercare di**

beach **la spiaggia**
sand **la sabbia**
sea, ocean **il mare, l'oceano**
land **la terra**
lighthouse **il faro**
wave **l'onda**
waves, ground swell, surf **i fran-genti, la risacca, il surf**
surfboard **la tavola da « surfing »**
surfing **il « surfing »**
ship **la nave**
float, air mattress **il materassino pneumatico**
sailboat **la barca a vela**
bathing suit **il costume da bagno**
bikini **il bikini**
(beach) mat **la stuoia**
shell **la conchiglia**
ball **il pallone, la palla**
hat **il cappello**
cap **il berretto**
bonnet **la cuffia, la cuffietta**
shovel **la pala**
pail **il secchio**

transistor radio **il transistore**
thermos jug **il thermos**
carry-all, totebag **la borsa**
sunglasses **gli occhiali da sole**
scarf **la sciarpa**
cup **la tazza**
binoculars **il binocolo**
beach umbrella **l'ombrello da spiaggia**
salt water **l'acqua salata**
fresh water **l'acqua dolce**
sunburn **la scottatura**
suntan lotion **la lozione per l'abbronzatura**

suntanned **abbronzato**
sunburned **scottato dal sole**
on one's head **in testa**
sometimes **qualche volta**

Alla spiaggia

Analisi del disegno

1. Ci sono due transistori nel disegno. Chi li hanno e dove sono?
2. Che pare voler fare la ragazzina dalla cuffia?
3. Chi porta un bikini?
4. Quali due cose sta cercando di fare simultaneamente la signora in primo piano di questo disegno?
5. Che crede Lei che si stiano raccontando il signore colla ragazzina e la signora con la sciarpa in testa?
6. Che sta guardando il signore che tiene il binocolo?
7. Chi tiene un materassino pneumatico? Dove pare che vada?
8. Che stanno facendo i ragazzi in fondo a sinistra del disegno?
9. Dove vede Lei una piccola barca a vela?
10. Chi porta occhiali da sole?
11. Che cose possono essere nella borsa della signora?
12. Dove ci sono conchiglie?
13. Dove stanno i thermos?
14. Che sta dicendo il ragazzo con il transistore alla ragazza in bikini?

Punti di partenza

15. Qual è la funzione di un faro?
16. Si può stare a galla meglio in acqua salata o in acqua dolce? Quale preferisce Lei?
17. Qual è la differenza tra un cappello e un berretto?
18. Come si può evitare una scottatura prendendo il sole?
19. Perchè è difficile qualche volta nuotare nel mare?
20. Perchè è facile o difficile per Lei andare alla spiaggia?

Temi per conversazione

1. La spiaggia (non) è per me.
2. Ciò che si può fare alla spiaggia.
3. Le tavole da « surfing » e facendo il « surfing ».

to cast a (fishing) line **lanciare la lenza**
to hunt (*game*) **cacciare**
to aim (*a gun*) **puntare**
to shoot (*a gun*) **sparare**
to cook **cucinare**
to climb **scalare**
to paddle **remare; pagaiare (una canoa)**
to sing **cantare**
to fish, to catch (*a fish*) **pescare**
to camp, to go camping **campeggiare**
to indicate **indicare**

outdoor life **la vita all'aperto**
campsite **il camping, il luogo di campeggio**
camp **il campo, il campeggio**
fisherman **il pescatore**

hunter **il cacciatore**
camper **il campeggiatore, la campeggiatrice**
hiker **il camminatore, la camminatrice**
canoeist **il canottiere**
fishing rod **la canna da pesca**
fishing line **la lenza**
reel **la bobina**
fly **la mosca**
fish **il pesce**
trout **la trota**
gun **il fucile**
game bag **il carniere**
deer **il cervo**
tent **la tenda di campagna**
skillet **la casseruola con lungo manico, la padella**
hike **l'escursione (*f.*) a piedi**
knapsack **lo zaino**
sky **il cielo**

mountain **la montagna, il monte**
top **la cima**
fire **il fuoco**
campfire (bonfire) **il falò**
sleeping bag **il sacco a pelo**
canoe **la canoa**
canoe paddle **la pagaia**
stream **il corrente**
bow (*of a boat*) **la prua**
stern (*of a boat*) **la poppa**
hat **il cappello**
season **la stagione (*dell'anno*)**
winter **l'inverno**
summer **l'estate (*f.*)**
spring **la primavera**
fall **l'autunno**

useful **utile**
red **rosso**
each one **ciascuno**

La vita all'aperto

Analisi del disegno

1. Che ci fa pensare che il pescatore sta lanciando una lenza per pescare trota?
2. Che può stare dicendosi il pescatore?
3. Che ha il pescatore sul suo cappello?
4. Che ci indica che il cacciatore non sta cacciando un cervo?
5. Nel disegno con la tenda di campagna, che sta facendo il campeggiatore?
6. Che ci può essere dentro la tenda di campagna?
7. Perchè può essere utile una casseruola con lungo manico per il pescatore?
8. Spieghi la differenza fra i due fuochi.
9. Chi stanno scalando la montagna?
10. Chi sta nella prua e chi sta nella poppa della canoa?
11. Di che cosa potrebbero stare parlando i canottieri?
12. Perchè possono essere le stesse le camminatrici ed il gruppo che sta cantando?
13. Che stanno facendo le campeggiatrici accanto al falò?
14. Quale delle sei scene preferisce Lei, e perchè?
15. Che metterebbe Lei in uno zaino per fare un'escursione a piedi di un giorno?

Punti di partenza

16. Quale Le sarebbe più utile, una canoa o un fucile? Perchè?
17. Con che si pagaia una canoa, con che si pesca e con che si caccia?
18. Perchè preferisce portare il rosso la maggioranza dei cacciatori?
19. Qual è la migliore stagione dell'anno per campeggiare? Perchè?
20. Quali sono le quattro stagioni dell'anno e che genere di vita all'aperto è più caratteristico per ciascuna?

Temi per conversazione

1. Come scegliere un luogo di campeggio.
2. I miei giorni in un campeggio.
3. Ciò che vidi dalla cima della montagna.

to swim **nuotare**
to dive **tuffarsi**
to drown **annegarsi**
to watch, to keep watch **vigilare**
to play **giocare**
to change one's clothes **cambiarsi i vestiti**
to undress **spogliarsi**
to have on (oneself) **portare, avere addosso**
to be about to **stare per**
to move **muovere, spostare**
to hear **sentire**

swimming pool **la piscina**
diving board **il trampolino**
deep end **l'estremità poco profonda**
ladder **la scala a pioli**
bathing suit **il costume da bagno**
cabana **la cabina balneare**
lifeguard **il bagnino**
crawl **il crawl**
backstroke **il nuoto sul dorso**
breaststroke **il nuoto a rana**

sunglasses **gli occhiali da sole**
whistle **il fischietto**
sandal **il sandalo**
hat **il cappello**
chaise longue **la sedia a sdraio**
softdrink **la gassosa, la bibita**
wheel **la ruota**
beach **la spiaggia**
age **l'età**

rapid, quick **veloce**

Alla piscina

Analisi del disegno

1. Dove sono le cabine balneari?
2. Come sa Lei che qualcuno sta per tuffarsi?
3. Quale di questi stili è il più veloce—a rana, sul dorso o crawl—e che stile sta usando la persona nella piscina?
4. Che suppone Lei che desideri il ragazzino? E che cosa gli starà dicendo il padre?
5. Di che cosa possono parlare, la signora con gli occhiali da sole ed il signore seduto sulla sedia a sdraio?
6. Chi sta bevendo una gassosa?
7. Perchè ha piccole ruote la sedia a sdraio?
8. Di chi sono i sandali?
9. Che sta facendo il bagnino?
10. Che ha addosso il bagnino?
11. In che estremità della piscina si trova la maggior parte della gente?
12. Perchè si trova la scala a pioli in quell'estremità?
13. Dove c'è un'altra scala?
14. In quale estremità della piscina stanno giocando i due ragazzini?
15. Perchè non ci sono ragazzini nell'estremità profonda?

Punti di partenza

16. Per che cosa si usa una cabina balneare?
17. Preferisce Lei andare alla piscina o alla spiaggia? Perchè?
18. Quali sono i compiti di un bagnino?
19. Perchè hanno le piscine un'estremità profonda e l'altra poco profonda?
20. Sa nuotare Lei? Se non lo sa, perchè no? Se lo sa, a che età ha cominciato a nuotare?

Temi per conversazione

1. Le piscine non sono fatte per nuotare.
2. Bagnini che ho conosciuti.
3. Conversazione sentita in una piscina.

to display **mostrare, esibire**
to consist of **consistere di**
to have in common **avere in comune**

men's shop **il negozio per signori**
for sale **in vendita**
on sale (*reduced price*) **in liquidazione**
clothing (*in general*), apparel **l'abbigliamento, i vestiti**
article of clothing **l'articolo di abbligliamento, l'indumento**
display window **la vetrina**
coat of arms **lo stemma (nobiliare)**
measurement **la misura**
suit **l'abito**
pants (*trousers*) **i calzoni, i pantaloni**

coat (*suit jacket*) **la giacca**
tie **la cravatta**
bow tie **il farfallino, la cravatta a farfalla**
shirt **la camicia**
sport shirt **la camicia sportiva**
long sleeves **le maniche lunghe**
short sleeves **le maniche corte**
cuff (*shirt*) **il polsino**
pocket **la tasca**
hip pocket **la tasca posteriore**
side pocket **la tasca laterale**
handkerchief **il fazzoletto**
underwear **la biancheria personale**
shorts **i calzoncini**
undershirt **la maglietta, la canottiera**
shoe **la scarpa**
socks **i calzini**
pair **il paio**

belt **la cintura**
billfold **il portafoglio**
cuff links **i bottoni da polsini, i gemelli**
tie clasp **la spilla da cravatta**
price tag **l'etichetta (del prezzo)**
pullover (*sweater*) **il maglione, il pullover**
jeans **i blue jeans**
shoelace **il laccio**
collar **il colletto**
button **il bottone**
leather **il cuoio**
monogram **il monogramma**
mannequin **il manichino**
hippie **il hippie, il capellone**

single-breasted **a un petto**
double-breasted **a doppio petto**

Il negozio per signori

Analisi del disegno

1. Quale articolo d'abbigliamento esibito nella vetrina costerà il meno?
2. Descriva l'abbigliamento del manichino con mani.
3. Descriva l'abbigliamento dei tre altri manichini.
4. Dov'è il monogramma sulla camicia sportiva?
5. Descriva gli articoli d'abbigliamento che non stanno sui manichini.
6. Qual è la differenza fra le scarpe del manichino e le altre scarpe?
7. C'è qualcosa che la maggioranza degli uomini porta ogni giorno che non si esibisce in questa vetrina. Che cos'è?
8. Crede Lei che lo stemma sia in vendita? Perchè
9. Descriva l'abbigliamento del hippie.
10. Che starà pensando il hippie?

Punti di partenza

11. Spieghi la differenza tra una giacca a un petto e una giacca a doppio petto.
12. Che cosa è un'etichetta?
13. Di che consiste un abito?
14. Di che consiste la biancheria personale di un uomo?
15. Che hanno in comune una cintura, un portafoglio e un paio di scarpe?
16. Quali indumenti da uomo hanno i bottoni?
17. Quante tasche ha un paio di calzoni?
18. Se un americano porta un abito, dove tiene il suo portafoglio? Se è europeo, dove lo tiene?
19. Per poter portare gemelli ed una spilla da cravatta, che tipo di camicia e quali altri articoli di abbigliamento si devono portare?
20. Quali sono le due misure che si devono sapere per comprare una camicia?

Temi per conversazione

1. Ciò che porto e ciò che non porto, e perchè.
2. Come mostrare articoli d'abbigliamento in una vetrina di un negozio per signori.
3. «La tonaca non fa il monaco». (Literally: "The cassock does not make the monk"; that is, "clothes do not make the man.")

to shop, to go shopping **fare delle compre**
to spend **spendere**
to charge **mettere sul conto aperto**
to pay cash **pagare in contanti**
to ring up a sale (*on the cash register*) **registrare una vendita**
to hold (*grasp, extend*) **tenere, estendere**
to try on **provare**
to fit one **andare bene**
to match **armonizzare (con), accompagnarsi**
to be right **avere ragione**
to look for **cercare**
to open **aprire**

department store **il gran magazzino**

counter **il banco di negozio**
cash register **il registratore di cassa**
salesman **il commesso**
saleslady **la commessa**
customer **il cliente, la cliente**
shopper **il compratore, la compratrice**
charge account **il conto aperto**
department **il reparto**
sale (*bargain*) **la liquidazione**
sale (*transaction*) **la vendita**
size **la taglia, la misura**
article of clothing or personal adornment **l'indumento**
mirror **lo specchio**
drawer **il cassetto**
scarf **la sciarpa**
jewelry **i gioielli**
necklace **la collana**

earring **il pendente** (*if it hangs*), **l'orecchino** (*ear post*)
bracelet **il braccialetto**
brooch **la spilla**
flower **il fiore**
purse **la borsa**
hose, stockings **le calze**
panty hose **il collant**
hat **il cappello**
glove **il guanto**
sweater **il maglione, il pullover**
blouse **la blusa**
fur coat **la pelliccia**
aisle **il corridoio**

only **unicamente**
up; on oneself **contro di sè**
on display **in mostra**
for sale **in vendita**

Il gran magazzino

Analisi del disegno

1. Dove sta la compratrice che non è accanto al banco?
2. Che sta cercando la commessa nel cassetto aperto?
3. Perchè non sta portando guanti la signora che sta davanti allo specchio?
4. Che cosa c'è in mostra sul banco del reparto di gioielli e in primo piano?
5. Perchè ci sono unicamente commesse e non commessi?
6. Che sta accadendo nel reparto di guanti?
7. È un pullover o una blusa ciò che tiene contro di sè la cliente? Perchè lo prova di questa maniera?
8. Che fa la commessa nel reparto di borse?
9. Come sa Lei che la borsa accanto allo specchio non è in vendita?
10. Dov'è il registratore di cassa e che sta accadendo lì?
11. Quali indumenti in questo disegno sarebbero difficili da comprare se la cliente non sapesse la sua misura?
12. Quale commessa porta qualcosa che lei stessa vende?

Punti di partenza

13. Qual è il vantaggio di avere un conto aperto?
14. Qual è il vantaggio di pagare in contanti?
15. Qual è la differenza tra una vendita ed una liquidazione?
16. Che è un gran magazzino?
17. « Il cliente ha sempre ragione ». Lo spieghi.
18. Perchè preferisce la maggior parte dei grandi magazzini negli Stati Uniti che i suoi clienti abbiano conti aperti?
19. Perchè Le piacerebbe, o perchè non Le piacerebbe, essere commesso (commessa) in un gran magazzino?
20. Alla maggioranza delle donne piace andare a fare delle compre nei grandi magazzini; alla maggioranza degli nomini non piace. Crede Lei che questo sia così? Perchè?

Temi di conversazione

1. Come scegliere una borsa.
2. Perchè il disegno della pagina anteriore è o non è autentico.
3. Come spenderei $1,000 in un gran magazzino.

to go grocery shopping **andare a comprare i commestibili o i generi alimentari**
to add (up) the bill **fare il conto**
to wait in line **fare la coda**
to weigh **pesare**
to slice **affettare; tagliare in fette**
to peel **pelare, sbucciare**
to resemble **somigliarsi**
to leave **lasciare**
to drop **far cadere, lasciar cadere**
to have just **avere appena** (*plus past participle*)
to collect **raccogliere**
to push **spingere**
to defrost **decongelare**
to melt **fondere, liquefarsi**

supermarket **il supermercato**
shopper **il compratore, la compratrice**
clerk **il venditore, la venditrice**

cashier, checker **il cassiere, la cassiera**
cash register **il registratore di cassa**
price **il prezzo**
purchase **la compra**
purse **la borsa**
counter **il banco**
groceries **i commestibili, i generi alimentari**
can **la latta, la scatola**
canned goods **lo scatolame, i prodotti in scatola**
bag, sack **la borsa per la spesa**
scale **la bilancia**
pushcart **il carrello**
kilo **il chilogrammo, il chilo,** (*2.2 libbre*)
pound **la libbra** (*.45 di un chilo*)
gallon **il gallone** (*3.78 litri*)
liter **il litro** (*.26 di un gallone*)
quart **il quarto di gallone** (*1.1 litri*)
fruit **la frutta**

vegetable **il legume**
milk **il latte**
meat **la carne**
apple **la mela**
banana **la banana**
peach **la pesca**
pear **la pera**
orange **l'arancio**
grapefruit **il pompelmo**
tomato **il pomodoro**
carrot **la carota**
celery **il sedano**
cabbage **il cavolo**
lettuce **la lattuga**
cauliflower **il cavolfiore**
spinach **gli spinaci**
leaf **la foglia**
apron **il grembiale**
pencil **la matita**
ear **l'orecchio**
week **la settimana**

frozen **congelato**

42

Il supermercato

Analisi del disegno

1. Che ha appena fatto il ragazzino?
2. Che commestibili ha già scelto la compratrice?
3. Chi sta portando un grembiale e che sta facendo?
4. Per che cosa usa il venditore la matita che ha all'orecchio?
5. Che cosa potremmo dedurre da questa scena se sapessimo che la bilancia pesa in libbre o in chili?
6. Che vede Lei in fondo a destra?
7. Che cosa fa con le mani la compratrice in primo piano?
8. Di che potrebbe stare pensando la compratrice in primo piano?

Punti di partenza

9. Chi compra i commestibili nella Sua famiglia e perchè?
10. Descriva qualche legume.
11. Descriva qualche frutta.
12. Che frutta in genere si tagliano in fette? Quali si sbucciano? Quali non si tagliano nè in fette nè si sbucciano?
13. In che si somigliano la lattuga e il cavolo?
14. Che è un cassiere di supermercato?
15. Perchè lascia la maggioranza della gente il banco della carne e quello dei legumi congelati fino all'ultimo momento?
16. Dove, e perchè si fa la coda in un supermercato?
17. Perchè Le piace (o non Le piace) comprare i commestibili?
18. Quando Le mettono le Sue compre in una borsa nel supermercato?
19. Dove si vende il latte al quarto di gallone e dove al litro?
20. Quali sono alcune cose che si possono comprare in scatola?

Temi per conversazione

1. I vantaggi e svantaggi relativi fra i prodotti in scatola e quei congelati.
2. La differenza tra un uomo ed una donna facendo compre in un supermercato.
3. Il supermercato americano.

to fill (make up, prepare) a prescription **preparare una ricetta**
to prescribe **ordinare; dare una ricetta**
to wait on (*a customer*) **servire**
to display **mostrare, esibire**
to take turns **fare il turno**
to smoke **fumare**
to chew **masticare**
to give (*information*) **fornire**

drugstore **la farmacia**
drugstore "on duty" **la farmacia aperta a turno**
druggist, pharmacist **il farmacista**
license (*to practice*) **la licenza**
prescription **la ricetta**
medicine **la medicina**
dose, dosage **la dose**

content(s) **il contenuto**
doctor, physician **il medico**
bottle **la bottiglia**
jar **il barattolo**
box **la scatola**
pill **la pillola**
aspirin **l'aspirina**
cosmetics **i cosmetici, i prodotti di bellezza**
bar of soap **il pezzo di sapone, la saponetta**
tube of toothpaste **il tubetto di pasta dentifricia**
stick of chewing gum **il pezzo di gomma da masticare**
pack (package) **il pacchetto**
carton (of cigarettes) **la stecca (di sigarette)**
cigarette **la sigaretta**
cigar **il sigaro**

perfume **il profumo**
toilet water, cologne **l'acqua di Colonia**
(bath) powder **il talco in polvere**
nail polish **lo smalto per le unghie**
shampoo **lo shampoo**
sunglasses **gli occhiali da sole**
shelf **lo scaffale**
label **l'etichetta**
soda fountain **il bar**
magazine **la rivista**
greeting card **la cartolina di auguri**
wall **la parete**
counter **il banco di negozio**

besides **oltre (a)**
instead of **invece di**

La farmacia

Analisi del disegno

1. Quali sono alcuni degli oggetti che si mostrano sugli scaffali?
2. Qual è il probabile contenuto della bottiglia che tiene nella mano la signora?
3. Che informazione fornirà alla signora l'etichetta che sta leggendo?
4. Che starà facendo il farmacista?
5. Quali sono le bottigliette di smalto per le unghie?
6. Perchè le medicine non sono sugli scaffali con i cosmetici?
7. Generalmente che altre cose si trovano in una farmacia americana oltre a quelle che si vedono in questo disegno?
8. Che si esibisce alla parete accanto alle medicine?
9. A chi crede Lei che stia servendo il farmacista e perchè è Lei di quest'opinione?

Punti di partenza

10. Dove si preparano le ricette? Chi le ordina?
11. Quante sigarette ci sono in un pacchetto e quante in una stecca?
12. Quanti pezzi ci sono in un pacchetto di gomma da masticare e quanto costa?
13. Dove non si deve nè masticare gomma da masticare nè fumare?
14. In Europa le farmacie stanno aperte a turno tutta la notte. Qual è la ragione di ciò?
15. In che cosa viene la pasta dentifricia? In che cosa vengono le pillole?
16. Qual è la differenza tra una sigaretta e un sigaro?
17. Nomini una pillola per la quale non bisogna avere una ricetta.
18. Che si può usare invece di shampoo?
19. Quali sono le cose in una farmacia che un uomo comprerebbe per se stesso e quali sono quelle che comprerebbe unicamente per una donna?
20. Che informazione ci fornisce l'etichetta di una scatola o bottiglia di medicina?

Temi per conversazione

1. La differenza tra una farmacia americana ed una farmacia europea.
2. I prodotti di bellezza.
3. Come scegliere le cartoline di auguri.

to bark **abbaiare**	pet shop **il negozio di animali domestici**	container **il recipiente**
to meow **miagolare**	Siamese cat **il gatto siamese**	paw **la zampa**
to sing **cantare**	kitten **il gattino**	claw **la grinfia, l'artiglio**
to climb **arrampicarsi (su per)**	dog **il cane**	ear **l'orecchio**
to sleep **dormire**	puppy **il cucciolo, il cagnolino**	tree **l'albero**
to eat (up) **mangiar(si)**	rabbit **il coniglio**	habitat **l'habitat** (*m.*)
to grow (up) **crescere**	bird **l'uccello**	head **la testa**
to take out **togliere**	canary **il canarino**	white hair **i capelli bianchi**
to fight **combattere**	cage **la gabbia**	saleslady **la commessa**
to escape **fuggire**	fish **il pesce**	wife **la moglie**
to catch **afferrare; prendere per mano**	tank (*for fish*) **l'acquario**	
to change into, to become **trasformarsi, diventare**	net **la rete**	old, elderly **anziano**
to need **avere bisogno (di)**	thermometer **il termometro**	expensive **caro**
	temperature **la temperatura**	inexpensive **poco costoso, meno caro, a buon mercato**
		cute **carino**

Il negozio di animali domestici

Analisi del disegno

1. Perchè crede Lei che l'anziano voglia comprare un pesce?
2. Crede Lei che l'anziana sia la moglie dell'anziano o la commessa? Perchè?
3. Dove c'è un termometro? Perchè?
4. Perchè servono il recipiente e la rete accanto all'acquario?
5. Dove vede Lei un gatto siamese?
6. In quale gabbia è il coniglio?
7. Qual è l'habitat naturale di ciascuno degli animali di questo disegno—aria, terra, acqua?
8. Quale crede Lei che sarebbe l'animale più caro e quale il meno caro?
9. Che stanno facendo i tre cuccioli?
10. Come sappiamo che la gabbia del canarino è davanti e non dietro all'anziana?
11. Quale degli animali del disegno sarà il più grande quando cresce?
12. Se tutti gli animali fossero liberi dentro il negozio, che succederebbe?

Punti di partenza

13. Quale specie di animale domestico preferisce Lei e perchè?
14. I cani abbaiano. Che fanno i gatti ed i canarini?
15. Nomini alcuni animali che hanno quattro zampe.
16. Che cosa è un acquario?
17. Di che ha bisogna un animale per poter arrampicarsi su per un albero?
18. Qual è la differenza tra un cucciolo e un cane?
19. Quali sono alcune somiglianze e differenze tra un cane, un gatto e un coniglio?
20. Che volle dire Ogden Nash quando scrisse che « l'unico problema con un gattino è che cresce e si trasforma in un gatto» ?

Temi per conversazione

1. Perchè, nella mia opinione, questo disegno è uno dei migliori (peggiori) di questo libro.
2. Perchè mi piacciono (o non mi piacciono) i gatti.
3. Ciò che si direbbero uno all'altro gli animali in un negozio di animali domestici se potessero parlare.

to drive (*a car*) **guidare, condurre**

to drive (*a given distance*) **viaggiare, percorrere**

to park **parcheggiare, posteggiare**

to blow (*a horn*) **suonare il clacson**

to work (*function*) **funzionare**

to sit **sedersi**

automobile **l'automobile** (*f.*), **la macchina**

engine **il motore**

driver **il conducente, il guidatore**

passenger **il passeggero, il viaggiatore**

front seat **il sedile anteriore**

rear seat **il sedile posteriore**

seat belt **la cintura (di sicurezza)**

steering wheel **il volante**

horn **il clacson**

windshield **il parabrezza**

windshield wiper **il tergi-cristallo**

hood **il cofano**

glove compartment **l'armadietto del cruscotto**

dashboard **il cruscotto**

clock **l'orologio**

heater **il riscaldatore**

air conditioning **l'aria condizionata**

radio **la radio**

button, knob **il bottone**

light **la luce**

pedal **il pedale**

accelerator, gas pedal **l'acceleratore** (*m.*)

starter, starting **la messa in moto**

brake **il freno**

emergency brake (*hand brake*) **il freno a mano**

clutch **la frizione**

automatic transmission **la trasmissione automatica**

standard (stick) transmission **il cambio a leva**

speed **la velocità**

speedometer **il tachimetro**

odometer **l'odometro**

mile **il miglio (le miglia,** *pl.*), (*1.60 chilometri*)

kilometer **il chilometro** (*.62 di un miglio*)

miles per hour **le miglia all'ora**

kilometers per hour **i chilometri all'ora**

door **lo sportello**

handle **la maniglia**

window **il finestrino**

electric window **il finestrino scorrevole elettrico**

rear-view mirror **lo specchio retrovisore**

eyeshade **il parasole**

armrest **il bracciolo**

ash tray **il portacenere**

through **attraverso**

to be cold **fare freddo**

to be hot **fare caldo**

L'automobile

Analisi del disegno

1. Come sa Lei che quest'automobile non ha finestrini elettrici?
2. Quali parti della macchina si possono vedere attraverso il parabrezza dall'interiore della macchina?
3. Dov'è il motore?
4. Che c'è fra i parasoli?
5. Che c'è sul cruscotto?
6. Quale pedale è a destra del freno?
7. Che cosa vede Lei sul sedile anteriore?
8. Per che cosa serve l'oggetto che è sopra il volante?
9. Perchè può fare caldo o freddo dentro questa macchina?
10. Che ha lo sportello di destra che non possiamo vedere su quello di sinistra?
11. Dove dovremmo star seduti per vedere ciò che si vede in questo disegno?
12. Come sa Lei che questa macchina ha la trasmissione automatica e non il cambio a leva?
13. Come sa Lei che questa macchina non è un modello nuovo?

Punti di partenza

14. Qual è la differenza tra un tachimetro ed un odometro?
15. Quando si usa il freno a mano?
16. Dove si siede il conducente? Dove si possono sedere i passeggeri?
17. Qual è l'equivalente in miglia se Lei guida a 100 chilometri all'ora?
18. Quanti chilometri ha viaggiato se Lei ha viaggiato 400 miglia?
19. Per che cosa usa lo specchio retrovisore un buon conducente?
20. Quali sono alcune delle cose che si possono tenere nell'armadietto del cruscotto?

Temi per conversazione

1. Descrizione dell'interiore di una macchina americana.
2. Come scegliere una macchina.
3. Come essere un buon conducente.

to get (put in) gasoline **mettere la benzina, rifornire**

to get (put in) water **mettere l'acqua**

to get (put in) air **gonfiare**

to lubricate, to grease **fare l'ingrassaggio, lubrificare**

to change the oil **cambiare l'olio**

to fill **riempire, fare il pieno**

to take **prendere**

to take a trip **fare un viaggio, andare in viaggio**

to cover a distance, to traverse **percorrere**

to turn on (*a light*) **accendere**

to start (*an engine*) **mettere in moto**

to turn off (*a light*), to stop (*an engine*) **spegnere**

to run (*said of an engine*) **essere in moto**

to drive **condurre, guidare**

to own **possedere, essere proprietario di**

to identify **identificare**

to hurt, to do harm to **danneggiare**

"to kill two birds with one stone" **« prendere due piccioni con una fava »** (to catch two pigeons with one bean)

service station, gas station **la stazione di servizio**

motorist, driver **il conducente, il guidatore**

passenger **il passeggero, il viaggiatore**

attendant **il benzinaio**

automobile, car **l'automobile (*f.*), la macchina**

engine **il motore**

sedan **la berlina**

coupé **il coupé**

convertible **la macchina decapottabile, lo spider**

station wagon **la giardinetta**

tire **la gomma, il pneumatico**

white-wall tire **la gomma con la banda bianca**

wheel **la ruota**

trunk **il portabagagli**

headlight **il faro**

tail light **il fanalino posteriore**

bumper **il paraurti**

pump **la pompa**

hose **il tubo di gomma**

license plate **la targa**

driver's license **il patente**

lubrication, "grease job" **la lubrificazione, il grassaggio**

grease gun **l'ingrassatore (*m.*)**

rack **la piattaforma**

battery **la batteria, l'accumulatore (*m.*)**

radiator **il radiatore**

crankcase **il carter**

seat **il sedile**

map **la carta**

tank **il serbatoio (per benzina)**

gallon **il gallone (*3.78 litri*)**

liter **il litro (*.26 di un gallone*)**

mile **il miglio (le miglia, *pl.*) (*1.60 chilometri*)**

kilometer **il chilometro (*.62 di un miglio*)**

oil **l'olio**

foreign **straniero**

La stazione di servizio

Analisi del disegno

1. Che sta facendo il benzinaio che è in primo piano?
2. Che cosa ci fa supporre che il guidatore stia per fare un viaggio?
3. Quali parti della macchina in primo piano può vedere Lei e che tipo di gomme ha?
4. Perchè si usano i due tubi di gomma di questo disegno?
5. Perchè potremmo dire che il benzinaio che è in primo piano sta prendendo due piccioni con una fava?
6. Perchè Le pare (o non Le pare) che sia straniera la macchina in primo piano di questo disegno?
7. Quali sono alcune differenze tra la macchina sulla piattaforma e la macchina che è accanto alla pompa?
8. Che tiene nella mano l'uomo che è sotto la piattaforma, e che sta facendo?

Punti di partenza

9. Per che cosa serve la targa? Il patente?
10. Dove si mette l'acqua in una macchina?
11. Se la benzina costa $.60 il gallone, quanto costa per riempire un serbatoio di 20 galloni di capacità?
12. Se Lei fa il pieno di un serbatoio di benzina con 52 litri, quanti galloni ha comprato?
13. Ogni quante miglia si cambia l'olio (del carter)?
14. Quali classi di servizio si possono avere in una stazione di servizio?
15. Quali sono alcune differenze tra una berlina, un coupé, una giardinetta ed una macchina decapottabile?
16. Perchè non si devono accendere i fari quando il motore è spento?
17. Perchè è difficile lubrificare una macchina se non si porta ad una stazione di servizio?
18. Se Lei è proprietario di una macchina, la descriva. Se non è proprietario di una macchina, perchè no?
19. Perchè ha più di una pompa la maggior parte delle stazioni di servizio?
20. A 15 miglia al gallone, quante miglia può Lei percorrere con 18 galloni di benzina nel serbatoio?

Temi di conversazione

1. Ciò che costa di essere proprietario di una macchina.
2. I compiti di un benzinaio.
3. Le donne (non) sono buone conducenti.

to check (*baggage*) **depositare**
to board **imbarcare**
to take off **decollare**
to fasten the seat belt **allacciar(si) la cintura di sicurezza**
to land **atterrare**
to pick up (*baggage*) **ritirare**
to smoke **fumare**
to lose **perdere**
to show **mostrare**
to wave **salutare con la mano**
to paint **dipingere**
to be about to **essere sul punto di**

airport **l'aeroporto**
airline **la linea aerea**
airplane **l'aeroplano, l'aereo**
jet **l'aviogetto, l'aeroplano a reazione**
pilot **il pilota**
stewardess, flight attendant **la hostess, l'assistente (*m. & f.*) di volo**
passenger **il passeggero**

flight **il volo**
ticket **il biglietto**
ticket office **la biglietteria**
reservation **la prenotazione**
list **la lista, l'elenco**
gate **la porta**
bording pass **la carta d'imbarco**
observation terrace **la terrazza d'osservazione**
control tower **la torre di controllo**
waiting room **la sala d'attesa**
suitcase **la valigia**
baggage **il bagaglio**
baggage inspection **l'ispezione (*f.*) dei bagagli**
baggage claim room **il deposito dei bagagli**
first class **la prima classe**
economy class **la classe turistica**
tourist **il turista**
customs **la dogana**
immigration **l'immigrazione (*f.*)**
documents (*passport, entry card, vaccination card, etc.*) **i documenti**
passport **il passaporto**
take-off **il decollo**
landing **l'atterraggio**
arrival **l'arrivo**
departure **la partenza**
cockpit **la carlinga**
engine **il motore**
wing **l'ala**
tail **la coda**
propeller **l'elica**
seat **il posto**
flag **la bandiera**
cart **il carrello**
baby **il bambino**

from **proveniente da**
to **con destinazione a**
international **internazionale**
domestic (*as opposed to international*) **nazionale**
stopped, standing, located **fermato**
since, inasmuch as **giacchè**

52

L'aeroporto

Analisi del disegno

1. Come sa Lei che questo è un aviogetto?
2. Quanti motori ha questo aereo? Come lo sa Lei?
3. Giacchè questo aeroplano ha una grande bandiera degli Stati Uniti dipinta sulla coda, quale classe di volo è probabile che sia?
4. Dove stanno i piloti e le assistenti di volo?
5. Come sa Lei che l'aereo è sul punto di decollare?
6. Quale passeggero è possibile che abbia problemi durante il volo? Perchè?
7. Chi sono le persone che si stanno salutando?
8. Chi non ha depositato una valigetta?
9. Che tiene nella mano l'uomo che sta in piedi accanto alla porta d'uscita?
10. Che c'è sul carrello?
11. Dov'è la terrazza d'osservazione?
12. Dove suppone Lei che si trovi la sala d'attesa?

Punti di partenza

13. Che deve fare e che non deve fare un passeggero durante il decollo e l'atterraggio?
14. Quali sono alcune differenze tra la prima classe e la classe turistica?
15. Dove ritira uno i suoi bagagli? Quando è necessaria l'ispezione dei bagagli?
16. In un volo proveniente da Nuova York con destinazione a Milano, dove, quando e a chi deve mostrare Lei i Suoi documenti nell'aeroporto di Milano?
17. Che è un turista?
18. Dove si fanno le prenotazioni e dove si comprano i biglietti?
19. Perchè non c'è la dogana negli aeroporti dove atterano solamente i voli nazionali?
20. Perchè non si deve tenere il passaporto nella valigia?

Temi per conversazione

1. Descrizione di un aeroplano (o aeroporto).
2. I servizi di una hostess.
3. Il giorno in cui la linea aerea perse i miei bagagli.

to take, to catch (*a train*) **prendere un treno**
to check (*baggage*) **depositare**
to claim **cercare, richiedere**
to travel **viaggiare**
to depart **partire**
to arrive **arrivare**
to stop **fermarsi**
to help **aiutare**
to eat **mangiare**
to browse, to leaf through **sfogliare**

railroad station **la stazione ferroviaria**
train **il treno**
freight train **il treno merci**
express train **il direttissimo**
local train **il locale, il treno ordinario**
locomotive **la locomotiva**
engineer **il macchinista**

conductor, ticket collector **il conduttore, il controllore**
porter **il facchino, il portabagagli**
ticket **il biglietto**
ticket window **lo sportello della biglietteria**
one-way ticket **il biglietto d'andata**
round-trip ticket **il biglietto d'andata e ritorno**
timetable **l'orario**
baggage **il bagaglio**
baggage check room **il deposito bagagli**
locker **l'armadietto per bagagli**
suitcase **la valigia**
passenger **il passeggero**
first class **la prima classe**
second class **la seconda classe**
third class **la terza classe**
pullman **la carrozza-salone**

diner **la carrozza-ristorante**
track **il binario**
cart **il carrello per bagagli**
newsstand **l'edicola, il chiosco**
magazine **la rivista**
overcoat **il soprabito**
arm **il braccio (le braccia, *pl.*)**
time (*clock time*) **l'ora**
time (*occasion*) **la volta, l'occasione (*f.*)**
little old lady **la vecchietta**
comparison **il paragone**

sometimes **talvolta**
instead of **invece di**
besides **oltre a**
nowadays **oggigiorno**
late **in ritardo**
early **in anticipo**
diesel **Diesel**
electric **elettrico**

La stazione ferroviaria

Analisi del disegno

1. Che tipo di locomotiva c'è sul binario?
2. Che tipo di locomotiva è più comune oggigiorno negli Stati Uniti?
3. Che sta facendo l'uomo che sta accanto all'edicola?
4. Descriva la vecchietta.
5. Che sta accadendo alla biglietteria?
6. Dove starà il facchino?
7. Che sta facendo il conduttore?
8. Che sta facendo l'uomo col soprabito sul braccio?
9. Quante valigie vede Lei e dove sta ciascuna di esse?

Punti di partenza

10. Che è un facchino? In che può aiutarLe un facchino?
11. Come si può viaggiare economicamente?
12. Che cose si possono fare in una stazione ferroviaria oltre al prendere un treno?
13. Dove si mangia in un treno?
14. In genere qual è il vantaggio di comprare un biglietto di andata e ritorno invece di uno di andata?
15. Perchè non c'è una carrozza-ristorante in un treno merci?
16. Che cosa è un orario?
17. Qual è la differenza principale tra un direttissimo ed un locale?
18. Dove deposita uno i suoi bagagli se è arrivato in anticipo e non desidera portare i bagagli da un lato all'altro della stazione?
19. Che luogo si può usare talvolta invece del deposito bagagli?
20. Se un treno arriva alle 7 di notte, come s'indica negli orari europei?

Temi per conversazione

1. Paragone fra treni europei ed americani.
2. Il treno è arrivato in ritardo questo giorno.
3. La storia della vecchietta.

to mail **spedire (per posta), imbucare**
to register or certify (*a letter*) **raccomandare**
to deliver **distribuire**
to weigh **pesare**
to collect **fare la levata**
to lose **perdere**
to delay, to take time **ritardare**
to look for **cercare**

post office **l'ufficio postale, la posta**
letter **la lettera**
postcard **la cartolina**
envelope **la busta**
stamp **il francobollo**
sheet of stamps **il foglio dei francobolli**
airmail **la posta aerea**
airmail stamp **il francobollo aereo**
special delivery **la consegna per espresso**

special delivery stamp **il francobollo per espresso**
commemorative stamp **il francobollo commemorativo**
mailbox, letter slot **la buca delle lettere, la cassetta per la posta**
regular mail (first-class) **la posta ordinaria**
ounce (*28.4 grams*) **l'oncia (le once, *pl.*)**
pound **la libbra**
package **il pacco**
postage **l'affrancatura**
rate **la tariffa**
domestic postage **l'affrancatura per l'interno**
foreign postage **l'affrancatura per l'estero**
address **l'indirizzo**
return address **il mittente**
postmark **il timbro postale**

postal meter **l'affrancatrice**
metered postage **l'affrancatura a stampa, l'affrancatura in abbonamento**
mailman (letter carrier) **il postino**
post office box **la casella postale**
home delivery **la distribuzione a domicilio**
general delivery **il fermo posta**
zip code **il codice postale**
C.O.D. **il pagamento alla consegna**
(clerk's) window **lo sportello**
purse **la borsa**
mouth **la bocca**
week **la settimana**

before **prima di**
red **rosso**
blue **azzurro**
green **verde**

L'ufficio postale

Analisi del disegno

1. Che sta facendo la signora in primo piano?
2. Perchè tiene le lettere in bocca la signora?
3. Chi tiene pacchi e dov'è questa gente?
4. Quale uomo non ha un pacco e che sta facendo?
5. Che fa la signora che sta a sinistra?

Punti di partenza

6. Quanto costa il francobollo per posta ordinaria negli Stati Uniti?
7. Che è una cartolina postale e quanto costa un francobollo per spedirla?
8. Che cosa vuol dire « pagamento alla consegna »?
9. Che colori su una busta indicano che va per posta aerea?
10. Che cosa vuol dire « affrancatura a stampa »?
11. Perchè costa di più l'affrancatura per l'estero che l'affrancatura per l'interno?
12. In quale giorno della settimana non c'è distribuzione a domicilio negli Stati Uniti?
13. Spieghi che cosa è « fermo posta »?
14. Che cosa indica il timbro postale?
15. Quanti grammi ci sono in una libbra?
16. Che differenza c'è tra posta ordinaria (« prima classe ») e le altre classi?
17. Su quale parte della busta si scrive l'indirizzo del mittente e perchè si scrive?
18. Per quale ragione si raccomandano le lettere?
19. Che cosa accade se si spedisce una lettera senza francobollo?
20. Perchè si pesa un pacco prima di spedirlo?

Temi per conversazione

1. I francobolli commemorativi americani.
2. Ciò che accade nell'ufficio postale.
3. Perchè mi piacerebbe (o non mi piacerebbe) essere postino.

to check in, to register **iscriversi**
to check out **andarsene**
to show to one's room **accompagnare alla camera**
to pay the bill **saldare il conto**
to stay (stop) at a hotel **fermarsi ad un albergo**
to clean the room **pulire la camera**
to request, to call for **chiedere**
to call **chiamare**
to receive **ricevere**

hotel **l'albergo, l'hotel**
motel **l'autostello, il motel**
room **la camera**
suitcase, bag **la valigia**
luggage, bags **il bagaglio**
front desk **la reception, il bureau**
desk clerk **il receptionist**
bellboy **il fattorino**
(hotel) guest **l'ospite** (*m. & f.*)
mail **la posta, la corrispondenza**
mailbox **la casella di posta**
set of mailboxes, pigeonholes **il casellario**
key **la chiave**
lobby **l'atrio, la hall, il vestibolo**
elevator **l'ascensore** (*m.*)
floor (*on which one walks*) **il pavimento**
floor (*story*) **il piano**
ground floor (main floor, first floor) **il pianterreno**
second floor (*European first floor*) **il primo piano**
maid (chambermaid) **la cameriera**
service **il servizio**
room service **il servizio in camera**
tip **la mancia (le mance,** *pl.*)
rug **il tappeto**
mirror **lo specchio**
fur coat **la pelliccia (le pellicce,** *pl.*)
hat **il cappello**
purse **la borsa**
arm **il braccio (le braccia,** *pl.*)
hand **la mano (le mani,** *pl.*)
logic **la logica**

usually **di solito**
unlucky **sfortunato**
outside of, aside from **fuori di**

L'albergo

Analisi del disegno

1. Quali oggetti Le fanno pensare che quest'albergo sia buono ed abbastanza grande?
2. Chi porta un cappello?
3. Quante valigie si vedono e dove sono?
4. Quanti ascensori ci sono e dove stanno?
5. Come sappiamo che gli ospiti stanno iscrivendosi e non andandosene dall'albergo?
6. Che cosa ha la signora sul suo braccio sinistro? Sul braccio destro? Nella mano sinistra?
7. Chi sta dando una chiave a chi? Perchè
8. Dov'è il casellario? Che c'è in alcune delle caselle?
9. Che si vede in fondo a destra?
10. Quanti fattorini può vedere Lei? Dove stanno? Che stanno facendo?

Punti di partenza

11. Di solito, quando si salda il conto in un albergo?
12. Quando e perchè si danno mance ai fattorini?
13. Quando e perchè è possibile chiedere « servizio in camera » ?
14. Perchè crede Lei che alcuni alberghi non usino il numero 13 nella numerazione delle camere?
15. Sa Lei che fuori degli Stati Uniti ciò che qui chiamiamo il primo piano è il pianterreno, che il nostro secondo piano è il loro primo piano, e così successivamente? Spieghi la logica di questi due sistemi.
16. Perchè non ha ascensori la maggior parte degli autostelli?
17. Chi pulisce la camera? Quando e con che frequenza la pulisce?
18. Come si dice in italiano "the rug on the floor of the third floor"?
19. Dove preferisce Lei fermarsi, ad un albergo o ad un autostello? Perchè?
20. Come si può ricevere corrispondenza in un albergo?

Temi per conversazione

1. Differenze tra un albergo ed un motel.
2. Il vestibolo dell'albergo.
3. Ciò che mi disse il fattorino.

MENU
RISTORANTE "TRE ROSE"

(Già Trattoria Franco)
Via Torino 18. Tel: 073.113
Proprietario: Gabriele Sardoni

ALLA CARTA

Antipasti	Lire
Piatto misto	900
Scampi all'aglio	850
Sardine sott'olio	400
Prosciutto con melone	750

Minestre
Minestra d'asparagi	350
Minestrone	300

Pasta
Lasagne verdi al forno	500
Spaghetti al pomodoro	400
Fettuccine al burro	500

Pesce
Pesce alla griglia	1.200
Filetti di sogliola	1.000

SERVIZIO COMPRESO

Specialità Della Casa	Lire
Pollo oreganato con insalata verde	1.600

Carne
Bistecca alla Fiorentina	2.200
Bistecca ai ferri	1.500
Agnello allo spiedino	1.400
Arrosto di maiale	1.000

Tutti i piatti sono serviti con contorno di verdura di stagione.

Formaggio	300
Frutta di stagione	200
Dolce	400
Gelato	400

PRANZI A PREZZO FISSO
(Servizio di 15% non-compreso)

A L. 2.500:

1 antipasto
Lasagne verdi al forno
Bistecca ai ferri . . o . . .
Agnello allo spiedino
Frutta e formaggio
Mezzo di Chianti

A L. 1.700:

Spaghetti al pomodoro
Arrosto di maiale
Frutta e formaggio
Quarto di vino da pasto

Vini

Chianti	800	Soave	1.300
Da pasto	600	Bardolino	1.300

---

to order **ordinare**
to eat **mangiare**
to go **andare**

restaurant **il ristorante, la trattoria** (*più modesta di un ristorante*)
menu **il menu, la lista, la carta**
tip **la mancia** (**le mance,** *pl.*)
meal **il pasto**
main meal, dinner **il pranzo**
hors d'oeuvre, appetizer **l'antipasto**
soup **la minestra, il minestrone**
fish **il pesce**
meat **la carne**
side dish (*vegetable*) **il contorno**
vegetable **la verdura**
cheese **il formaggio**
dessert (*cake, sweet*) **il dolce**
ice cream **il gelato**
prawn **lo scampo**
salad **l'insalata**
tomato **il pomodoro**
chicken **il pollo**
ham **il prosciutto**

asparagus **l'asparago**
(flour dough) meal(s) **la pasta, la pasta asciutta**
"pasta" meals **le lasagne, gli spaghetti, le fettuccine**
wine **il vino**
steak **la bistecca**
grill **la griglia**
sole (*fish*) **la sogliola**
pork **il maiale**
roast **l'arrosto**
lamb **l'agnello**
skewer **lo spiedino**
plate, dish **il piatto**
butter **il burro**
name **il nome**
cooking **la cucina**
course (*of a meal*) **la portata, la pietanza**
lire *Italian monetary unit: 650 Lire (L.) = approximately $1.00*
quarter (*of liter*) **il quarto**
half (*of liter*) **il mezzo**
country **il paese**

mixed, assorted **misto**

green **verde**
rare (*of meat*) **poco cotto, al sangue**
medium (*of meat*) **non troppo cotto**
well-done (*of meat*) **ben cotto**
firm (*to taste of « pasta » meals*) **al dente**
in the Florentine style **alla Fiorentina**
luxurious **di lusso**
seasonal **di stagione**
often **spesso**
outside of **fuori di**
table d'hôte, meal at a fixed price **pranzo a prezzo fisso**
included **compreso**
formerly **già**
prepared with oregano (*spice*) **oreganato**
prepared in oil **sott'olio**
prepared in garlic sauce **all'aglio**
a la carte **alla carta, a volontà**
roasted, baked **al forno**
grilled **ai ferri**
average **medio**

Il menu

Analisi del disegno

1. Che cosa vuol dire « alla carta » ?
2. Che significa « pranzo a prezzo fisso » ?
3. Che cos'è «antipasto»?
4. Che cosa vuol dire l'espressione « servizio compreso » ?   « Servizio non-compreso » ?
5. Dal menu del disegno, che idea ha Lei della quantità e della varietà di un pranzo italiano?
6. Se Lei ordinasse un pranzo alla carta da questo menu, quale sarebbe e quanto costerebbe?
7. Quale pietanza del menu si potrebbe ordinare « al dente » ?
8. Che cosa vuol dire « specialità della casa » ?

Punti di partenza

9. Quando si paga di più normalmente–quando si mangia « alla carta » o « a prezzo fisso »? Perchè?
10. Quanti diversi piatti di pasta ha mangiato Lei in vita Sua? Li nomini.
11. Come preferisce la bistecca–al sangue, non troppo cotta o ben cotta?
12. Gli Italiani usano molto l'aglio e l'olio nella loro cucina. Che pensa Lei di quest'uso?
13. Quanto è in dollari, approssimativamente, un pranzo a prezzo fisso di L. 1.700? Di L. 2.500?
14. Quale nome darebbe Lei ad un ristorante o ad una trattoria se avesse l'opportunità di farlo?
15. Quanto spesso mangia Lei nei ristoranti italiani?   Dove sono?
16. Se Lei andasse a mangiare in un ristorante di lusso, con chi vorrebbe andare e chi pagherebbe?
17. In genere dove crede Lei che mangino le famiglie italiane medie quando mangiano fuori di casa? Perchè?
18. Dove crede Lei che si paghi di più per mangiare un pranzo–in un ristorante o in una trattoria? Perchè?
19. Che cosa contiene, o può contenere, una pizza?
20. Quale paese europeo è molto famoso per la sua cucina?

Temi per conversazione

1. Un buon ristorante dove ho mangiato recentemente.
2. Qualche differenza tra un menu italiano ed un menu americano.
3. Perchè mi piace (non mi piace) la cucina italiana.

to spend **spendere**
to save **risparmiare, fare risparmi**
to pay **pagare**
to maintain, to keep **mantenere**
to review **riesaminare, rivedere**
to predict, to foresee **predire, prevedere**
to exceed **superare**
to need **avere bisogno (di)**

family budget **il bilancio familiare**
income **il reddito**
expenditure, expense **la spesa**
incidental expenses **le spese casuali**
money **il denaro**
payment **il pagamento**
down payment **l'acconto**
purchase **la compra, l'acquisto**
installment purchase **la compra a rate**
amount **la somma**
bill **il conto**

salary **lo stipendio**
dollar **il dollaro**
checkbook **il libretto d'assegni**
bank **la banca**
charge account **il conto aperto**
checking account **il conto corrente**
career **la carriera**
rent **l'affitto, il pigione**
mortgage **l'ipoteca**
utilities **i servizi**
tax, taxes **l'imposta, le imposte**
insurance **l'assicurazione** (*f.*)
interest **l'interesse** (*m.*)
transportation **il trasporto**
clothes, clothing **i vestiti, l'abbigliamento**
food, groceries **i generi alimentari**
entertainment **il divertimento**
vacation **la vacanza, le vacanze**
pocket money, spending money **il denaro per le piccole spese**
allowance **l'indennità**
year **l'anno**
month **il mese**

week **la settimana**
father **il padre**
mother **la madre**
husband **il marito**
wife **la moglie**
(married) couple **la coppia (sposata), i coniugi**
father and mother, parents **i genitori**
baby, child **il bambino, la bambina**
crib **il lettino a sbarre**
bedroom **la camera da letto**
table **la tavola**
lamp **la lampada**
pencil **la matita**
sheet of paper **il foglio di carta**

daytime **di giorno**
nighttime **di notte**
medical **medico**
dental **dentale**
monthly **mensile**
young **giovane**
how much? **quando?**

62

Il bilancio famigliare

Analisi del disegno

1. Che cosa vede Lei dentro la camera da letto?
2. Crede Lei che sia di giorno o di notte? Perchè?
3. Nomini gli oggetti che sono sulla tavola.
4. Che potrebbe dire il marito a sua moglie?
5. Che potrebbe rispondere la moglie a suo marito?
6. Che cosa suppone Lei che sia il problema principale del bilancio di questi genitori che stanno riesaminando le loro spese?
7. Perchè questa coppia ha bisogno di un bilancio?
8. Se non hanno altri bambini, quanto crede Lei che la coppia nel disegno spenda ogni settimana per i generi alimentari?
9. Inventi un bilancio mensile per tutte le spese della coppia che si vede nel disegno.

Punti di partenza

10. Che cosa è un bilancio?
11. Qual è il vantaggio di mantenere un bilancio?
12. Ha Lei un bilancio per le Sue spese personali? Se sì, perchè? Se no, perchè no?
13. Qual è la Sua spesa mensile più grande?
14. Se le Sue spese superano il Suo reddito, quali sono alcune delle soluzioni possibili?
15. Se Lei facesse risparmi settimanalmente per cinque anni, quanto denaro avrebbe nella banca?
16. Quali sono alcune spese tipiche e necessarie nel bilancio mensile di una tipica, giovane coppia sposata?
17. Non tutte le spese possono essere previste. Ne nomini una o due.
18. Spieghi che cos'è una compra a rate.
19. Quali sono i vantaggi e gli svantaggi di usare conti aperti?
20. Che cos'è « pocket money »?

Temi per conversazione

1. Il mio bilancio personale.
2. Come fare risparmi di denaro.
3. Le madri giovani (non) dovrebbero avere carriere.

to pay **pagare**
to receive **ricevere**
to lend **prestare**
to borrow **prendere in prestito**
to deposit **depositare**
to withdraw **prelevare**
to open an account **aprire un conto**
to cash (*a check*) **incassare**
to earn **guadagnare**
to spend **spendere**
to fill out (*a form*) **riempire**
to invest **investire**
to form a line (*of people*) **fare la coda**
to sign **firmare**
to function, to work **funzionare**
to forget **dimenticare**
to refer to **.riferirsi a**
to think, to intend **pensare**
to lose **perdere**
to sit down **sedersi**
to rain **piovere**

bank **la banca, il banco**
banker (*officer of a bank*) **il banchiere**
bank employee **l'impiegato di banca**
teller **il cassiere, la cassiera**
teller's window **lo sportello**
cash **i contanti**
money **il denaro**
banking hours **l'orario di banca**
loan **il prestito**
interest **l'interesse** (*m.*)
mortgage **l'ipoteca**
deposit slip **il modulo di deposito**
withdrawal slip **il modulo di prelevamento**
check **l'assegno, il cheque**
checkbook **il libretto d'assegni**
checking account **il conto corrente**
traveler's check **l'assegno turistico**
bank book (passbook) **il libretto di cassa**

savings account **il conto di cassa**
safe, vault **la cassaforte**
safe-deposit box **la cassetta di sicurezza**
bill (*money due*) **il conto**
bill (*banknote*) **il biglietto**
wallet **il portafoglio**
purse (*lady's*) **la borsa**
customer **il cliente**
guard **la guardia**
share of stock **l'azione** (*f.*)
stock market **la borsa**
umbrella **l'ombrello**
sign **l'indizio, l'avviso**
writing table, desk **lo scrittoio**
waste basket **il cestino per la carta straccia**
ledge **la mensola**
time (*occasion*) **la volta, l'occasione**

soon, shortly **fra poco, fra breve**
today **oggi**

La banca

Analisi del disegno

1. Quante persone ci sono nella banca? Quanti clienti si possono vedere?
2. Chi crede che pioverà e perchè?
3. Di che cosa possono stare parlando le persone che stanno sedute?
4. Dov'è il cestino per la carta straccia?
5. Crede Lei che gli impiegati della banca andranno a casa fra poco? Qual è la ragione per la Sua opinione?
6. Dove hanno fatto la coda i clienti?
7. Che crede Lei che stia facendo la gente che sta allo scrittoio situato al centro della banca?
8. Chi ha dimenticato qualche cosa? Che cosa ha dimenticato? Dov'è?
9. A che si riferisce il 5% dell'indizio?
10. Dov'è il cassiere?
11. Dov'è la guardia?

Punti di partenza

12. Quanto denaro ha Lei oggi nel Suo portafoglio e per quali cose lo vorrebbe spendere?
13. Come si deposita e come si preleva denaro in una banca?
14. Qual è il vantaggio di un conto corrente?
15. Qual è l'orario tipico di una banca?
16. Quando andò Lei alla banca l'ultima volta e per che cosa andò?
17. Che è interesse? Quando si riceve?
18. Qual è il vantaggio di assegni turistici?
19. Come si incassa un assegno?
20. Quali sono i vantaggi e gli svantaggi della vita di un banchiere?

Temi per conversazione

1. Come funziona una banca.
2. I vantaggi e gli svantaggi d'avere una cassetta di sicurezza.
3. Come io investirei denaro se ne avessi.

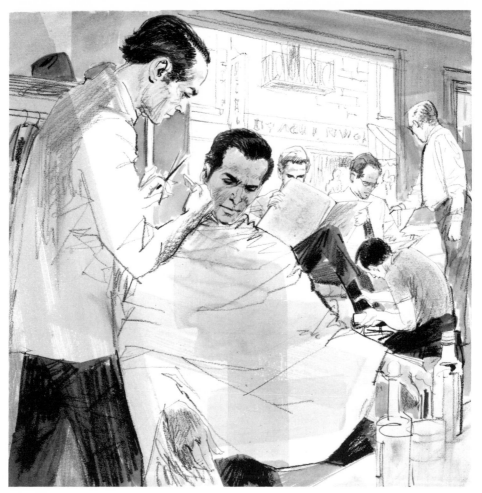

to cut hair **tagliare i capelli**
to get a haircut **andare a farsi tagliare i capelli**
to shave (oneself) **farsi la barba, radersi**
to get a shave **andare a farsi fare la barba**
to shine shoes **lustrare scarpe**
to get a shoeshine **andare a farsi lustrare le scarpe**
to comb **pettinare**
to wait one's turn **aspettare il turno**
to be on one's feet **stare in piedi**

at the barbershop **dal barbiere, dal parrucchiere**
barbershop **il negozio di bar-**

biere (parrucchiere)
barber **il barbiere, il parrucchiere**
customer **il cliente**
hair **i capelli**
haircut **il taglio dei capelli**
comb **il pettine**
scissors **le forbici**
shave **la barba**
shaving cream **la crema da barba**
lather **la saponata**
razor **il rasoio**
razor blade **la lametta**
straight razor, barber's razor **il rasoio a mano libera**
safety razor **il rasoio di sicurezza**
electric razor **il rasoio elettrico**

clippers **la macchinetta**
beard **la barba**
whiskers **le fedine, i favoriti**
moustache **i baffi**
sideburns **le basette**
soap **il sapone**
apron **la mantiglia**
newspaper **il giornale**
coat rack **l'attaccapanni** (*m.*)
hat rack **il portacappelli**
barber's pole **il palo dei barbieri**

left-handed **mancino, che usa la mano sinistra**
while **mentre**
red **rosso**
white **bianco**
Spanish, Spaniard **spagnolo**

Dal barbiere

Analisi del disegno

1. Che fa il barbiere in questo disegno?
2. Perchè si mette una mantiglia sopra il cliente?
3. Chi si sta facendo lustrare le scarpe?
4. Come sa Lei che il barbiere è mancino?
5. Dove vede Lei un cappello?
6. Che c'è sotto il portacappelli?
7. Che cosa vede Lei in fondo del disegno?

Punti de partenza

8. Di quali colori è il palo dei barbieri?
9. Con che preferisce Lei farsi la barba, con un rasoio a mano libera, con un rasoio di sicurezza o con un rasoio elettrico? Perchè?
10. Perchè deve stare in piedi la maggior parte del giorno il parrucchiere?
11. Con che frequenza va Lei a farsi tagliare i capelli?
12. Quanto paga Lei per un taglio dei capelli?
13. Quanto costa per farsi lustrare le scarpe?
14. Che cosa si può fare mentre si aspetta il turno in un negozio di barbiere?
15. Che sono le basette?
16. Quando usa il parrucchiere la macchinetta?
17. In quale famosa opera italiana c'è un barbiere spagnolo?
18. Che cosa è una barba? Che sono i baffi?
19. Qual è la Sua opinione dei baffi e dei favoriti?
20. Come si può fare la barba senza saponata?

Temi per conversazione

1. Come farsi la barba con un rasoio di sicurezza.
2. Come tagliare i capelli.
3. Descrizione di un negozio di barbiere.

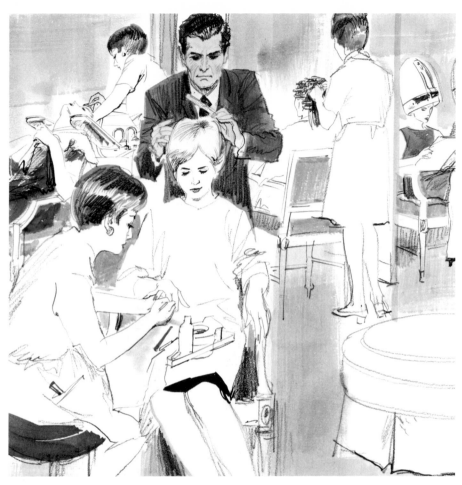

to cut **tagliare**
to wash **lavare**
to rinse **sciacquare**
to set **fare la messa in piega**
to dry **asciugare**
to comb (out) **pettinare**
to roll on curlers **mettere i bigodini**
to take off curlers **togliere i bigodini**
to bleach **scolorire**
to tease (*hair*) **cotonare**
to manicure **fare la manicure**
to have on (oneself) **portare, portare addosso**
to need **avere bisogno (di)**
to think about **pensare a**

beauty parlor **il salone di bellezza**

beautician (*hair dresser*) **il parrucchiere, la parrucchiera**
head **la testa**
hair **i capelli**
hair style **la pettinatura**
"set" **la messa in piega**
curly hair **i capelli ricci**
wavy hair **i capelli ondulati**
straight hair **i capelli lisci**
braid **la treccia**
shampoo **lo shampoo**
dryer **il casco asciugacapelli**
comb **il pettine**
curler **il bigodino**
hairpin **la forcina da capelli**
bobby pin **la molletta**
manicure **la manicure**
manicurist **la manicure**
finger nail **l'unghia**
finger nail file **la lima da unghie**

nail polish **lo smalto per le unghie**
nail polish remover **l'acetone** (*m.*)
gown, smock **il camiciotto**
earring **il pendente** (*if it hangs*), **l'orecchino** (*ear post*)
tray **il vassoio**
bottle **la bottiglia**
customer **il cliente, la cliente**

blonde **bionda**
brunette **bruna**
redhead **rossa**
sure, certain **sicuro**
what do you think of . . .?
  come Le pare . . .?
how long does it take to . . .?
  quanto tempo ci vuole per . . .?
now, nowadays **ora, oggigiorno**

68

Il salone di bellezza

Analisi del disegno

1. Che sta facendo il parrucchiere alla signora?
2. Descriva ciò che sta succedendo in fondo a sinistra.
3. Quali clienti già hanno i capelli lavati?
4. Che c'è nella bottiglia che è nel vassoio?
5. Perchè non ha bisogno di un pettine nel vassoio la manicure?
6. Chi non porta un camiciotto?
7. Quale delle clienti è probabilmente da più lungo tempo nel salone di bellezza? Perchè?
8. Di quali persone nel disegno possiamo essere sicuri che non portano pendenti?
9. Come Le pare lo stile di pettinatura della signora che stanno pettinando?

Punti partenza

10. Perchè vanno le donne al salone di bellezza?
11. Nel salone di bellezza, che fa la parrucchiera prima di fare la messa in piega?
12. Che accade quando son stati messi i bigodini?
13. Quando si tolgono i bigodini?
14. Che Le piace di meno: il lavare, la messa in piega o l'asciugare dei capelli? Perchè?
15. Preferisce Lei un parrucchiere o una parrucchiera? Perchè?
16. A che pensa Lei quando ha il casco asciugacapelli sopra la testa?
17. Che cosa è una manicure?
18. Che può fare una bruna che vuol essere una bionda o una rossa?
19. Quanto tempo ci vuole per asciugarsi i capelli?
20. Quando si usano le forcine da capelli e quando si usano delle mollette?

Temi per conversazione

1. Descrizione di un salone di bellezza.
2. Le pettinature d'oggigiorno.
3. La mia pettinatura è un problema.

to get sick **ammalarsi, cader ammalato**
to treat (*an illness*) **curare**
to take (one's) pulse **tastare il polso**
to take (one's) temperature **prendere la temperatura**
to bandage **bendare, fasciare**
to suffer **soffrire**
to live **vivere**
to die **morire**
to wear, to have on or with oneself **portare**
to listen (to) **ascoltare**

hospital **l'ospedale** (*m.*)
infirmary **l'infermeria, il dispensario**
doctor (physician) **il medico**
nurse **l'infermiera**
patient **il paziente, la paziente**

private room **la camera individuale, la camera privata**
semiprivate room **la camera semiprivata**
ward **la corsia**
medicine **la medicina**
sickness, disease **la malattia**
injury, wound **la ferita**
bandage **la benda, la fascia**
medical insurance **l'assicurazione medica, l'assicurazione contro l'invalidita**
inoculation **l'inoculazione** (*f.*)
visiting hours **le ore di visita, l'orario delle visite**
visitor **il visitatore, la visitatrice**
smallpox **la varicella**
heart **il cuore**
heart attack **l'infarto, l'accesso cardiaco**

stethoscope **lo stetoscopio**
thermometer **il termometro**
chart **la cartella clinica**
wristwatch **l'orologio di polso**
sheet **il lenzuolo**
bed **il letto**
night table **il tavolino da notte, il comodino**
tray **il vassoio**
flower **il fiore**
arm **il braccio (le braccia,** *pl.***)**
wrist **il polso**
smock, white gown **il camiciotto, il camice**
accident **l'incidente** (*m.*)

sick **ammalato, malato**
healthy **sano**
grave, serious **grave**
nowadays **oggigiorno**

L'ospedale

Analisi del disegno

1. Che sta facendo l'infermiera?
2. Che sta facendo il medico?
3. Perchè crede Lei che sia più probabile che questo paziente soffra di una ferita e non di una malattia?
4. Dove ci sono fiori ed un vassoio di medicine?
5. Perchè suppone Lei che l'infermiera porti un orologio di polso?
6. Descriva il medico.
7. Come sa Lei che il paziente di questo disegno non è morto?
8. Perchè non si può vedere il braccio destro del paziente?

Punti di partenza

9. Perchè molta poca gente si ammala della varicella oggigiorno?
10. Qual è la differenza principale tra un ospedale ed un dispensario?
11. Per che cosa si usa lo stetoscopio?
12. Che cosa è una corsia? Una camera individuale? Una camera semiprivata?
13. Chi sono le persone sane che si vedono in un ospedale?
14. Spieghi ciò che vuol dire « assicurazione medica ».
15. Che significa la frase « ore di visita » ?
16. Perchè preferiscono tutti essere visitatori e non pazienti?
17. Se Lei avesse una malattia grave, perchè sarebbe meglio andare ad un ospedale prima di farsi curare in casa?
18. Come si tasta il polso?
19. Quanti anni può vivere l'uomo oggigiorno?
20. Perchè è molto grave un accesso cardiaco?

Temi per conversazione

1. Il mio incidente (o la mia malattia).
2. Come prendersi la temperatura e come interpretarla.
3. Il dispensario della nostra università.

to persuade **persuadere, convincere**
to sway **dissuadere**
to speak, to address oneself to **indirizzarsi a**
to give a speech **pronunciare un discorso**
to debate **dibattere, discutere, deliberare**
to preach **predicare**
to vote **votare**
to choose **scegliere**
to agree **essere d'accordo**
to disagree **non essere d'accordo**
to go on strike **scioperare, fare lo sciopero**
to be on strike **essere in sciopero**
to assure **assicurare**
to listen (to) **ascoltare**
to try (to) **cercare (di)**
to feel, to sense **sentire**
to work **lavorare**
to write **scrivere**

persuasion **la persuasione**
vote **il voto**
voter **il votante, l'elettore** (*m.*)
voting booth **la cabina elettorale**
voting machine **la macchina per votare**
ballot **la scheda**
candidate **il candidato**
election **l'elezione** (*f.*)
curtain **la tendina**
privacy **la secretezza**
policeman **l'agente** (*m.*) **di polizia, il poliziotto**
factory **la fabbrica**
worker **l'operaio**
union (*of workers*) **il sindacato**
sign **il cartello**
fence **il recinto**
side **il lato**
student **lo studente, la studentessa**
student leader **il leader studentesco**
speech **il discorso**
debate **il dibattito**

speaker **l'oratore** (*m.*)
microphone **il microfono**
campus **la città universitaria**
building **l'edificio (gli edifici, *pl.*)**
meeting **la riunione**
convention **il congresso**
congregation **la congregazione**
politician **il politico**
judge **il giudice**
lawyer, attorney **l'avvocato**
courtroom **il tribunale**
robe **la toga**
party (*political*) **il partito**
right (*privilege*) **il diritto**
rightness (*state of being right*) **la rettitudine**
clergyman **l'ecclesiastico**
pulpit **il pulpito**
sermon **il sermone**

democratic **democratico**
republican **repubblicano**
extemporaneous **improvvisato**
above, up, upper **sopra**
each (one) **ciascuno**
both...and **sia...che**

La persuasione

Analisi del disegno

1. Perchè ha una tendina la cabina elettorale?
2. Perchè c'è un agente di polizia accanto alla cabina elettorale?
3. Che c'è all'altro lato del recinto?
4. Perchè porta il cartello l'operaio?
5. Che ci fa supporre che il disegno di sopra a destra rappresenti una riunione in una città universitaria?
6. Che fa il leader studentesco? Crede Lei che gli studenti siano d'accordo con lui?
7. Che edifici si possono vedere nei sei disegni?
8. Quale sarebbe la differenza fra i discorsi del leader studentesco e quelli del politico?
9. Dov'è l'avvocato e con chi sta deliberando?
10. Quali persone portano toghe nei disegni?
11. Da dove parla l'ecclesiastico e a chi s'indirizza?
12. Sia la signora che esce dalla cabina elettorale e l'uomo che porta il cartello hanno votato. Per che cosa ha votato ciascuno?
13. Spieghi di che cosa sta cercando di convincere la gente uno degli oratori.

Punti di partenza

14. Fra quali due grandi partiti può scegliere il votante americano?
15. Che cosa è un sindacato?
16. Che vuol dire « fare lo sciopero »?
17. Che differenza c'è tra « riunione », « congresso », e « congregazione »?
18. Qual è la differenza tra « predicare » e « dibattere » o tra un « sermone » e un « dibattito »?
19. Qual è la somiglianza tra un ecclesiastico, un politico ed un avvocato? Quali sono alcune differenze tra di loro?
20. Qual è il vantaggio (e svantaggio?) tra la macchina per votare e la scheda scritta?

Temi per conversazione

1. Il diritto di persuasione.
2. « Convinciti e convincerai ».
3. Gli studenti hanno (non hanno) il diritto di scioperare.

to advertise **annunciare; fare pubblicità**
to spend (*money*) **spendere**
to spend (*the night*) **pernottare**
to seek **cercare**
to translate **tradurre**
to qualify, to have the qualifications **qualificare**
to be worthwhile, to pay **valere la pena**
to place **collocare**
to post (*a sign*) **affissare**
to express **esprimere**
to address, to write to **indirizzare**

advertising, publicity **la pubblicità, la reclame, la propaganda**
advertisement **l'annuncio, l'avviso**
billboard **il cartellone pubblicitario**
highway **l'autostrada**
text **il testo**
hotel **l'albergo**
newspaper **il giornale**
classified ad(s) **la piccola pubblicità**
want ad **l'offerta (la domanda) di lavoro**

placement (*of ad*) **l'inserzione (f.)**
position, job **il posto, l'impiego**
housemaid **la domestica, la cameriera**
maid (*who takes care of clothing*) **la guardarobiera**
caretaking **la custodia**
caretaker **il custode**
domestic tasks **i lavori domestici**
married couple **i coniugi, la coppia**
health **la salute**
garden **il giardino**
agency **l'agenzia**
weekend **il (la) fine settimana, il weekend**
morning **la mattinata**
(household) helper **la collaboratrice**
country (*rural area*) **la campagna**
lake **il lago**
radio announcer **l'annunciatore di radio**
script **il copione**
magazine **la rivista**

television announcer **l'annunciatore di televisione**
television set **il televisore**
commercial **l'annuncio pubblicitario, la pubblicità**
slogan **il motto pubblicitario, lo slogan**
manner **il modo**

wanted (*in want ad*) **cercasi**
advertising **pubblicitario**
refined **signorile**
effective **efficace**
appropriate **adatto**
current, common, well-known **corrente**
full-page **a pagina intera**
with (letter of) recommendation **referenziato, con referenze, con la lettera di raccomandazione**
free **libero**
just **appena**
liking **amante**
permanent, "live-in" **fisso**
by means of **mediante**
in accordance with **secondo**
-self **stesso** (*when placed after the noun or pronoun*)

La pubblicità

Analisi del disegno

1. Perchè è (o non è) l'autostrada un luogo adatto per collocare un cartellone pubblicitario come quello del disegno?
2. Perchè è male (o bene) collocato il cartellone dell'autostrada?
3. Inventi un testo per l'annuncio del cartellone pubblicitario stradale.
4. Traduca in inglese le inserzioni di piccola pubblicità.
5. Per quale dei posti delle inserzioni di offerte di lavoro sarebbe (o non sarebbe) Lei qualificato?
6. Che starà leggendo l'annunciatore di radio dal suo copione?
7. Descriva l'annuncio della rivista.
8. Secondo ciò che vede al televisore, inventi un annuncio commerciale.
9. Completi il resto dell'annuncio dell'autobus.

Punti di partenza

10. Che è la piccola pubblicità?
11. Inventi un'inserzione di offerta di lavoro per il quale Lei stesso sarebbe qualificato.
12. Che cosa è un copione?
13. Che è un annuncio commerciale?
14. Nomini alcuni modi di fare pubblicità per un prodotto.
15. Perchè pare essere più difficile essere annunciatore di televisione che annunciatore di radio?
16. « Vale la pena di fare pubblicità ». Spieghi questa frase.
17. Perchè è l'autobus un buon luogo per affissare un avviso?
18. Come si sa se un annuncio è stato efficace o no?
19. Un modo di fare pubblicità è mediante l'uso di motti pubblicitari. Esprima in italiano alcuni motti di uso corrente negli Stati Uniti.
20. Quali categorie di prodotti si annunciano più frequentemente alla televisione?

Temi per conversazione

1. L'importanza di fare pubblicità.
2. Perchè la parola « propaganda » è difficile da tradurre dall'italiano in inglese e viceversa.
3. Inventi un annuncio a pagina intera di un prodotto per una rivista.

to publish **pubblicare**
to edit **redigere**
to compose **comporre**
to correct **correggere**
to type **scrivere a macchina, dattilografare**
to telephone **chiamare per telefono, telefonare**
to think of (*have an opinion of*) **pensare di**

editorial room, newspaper office **l'ufficio di redazione**
newspaper **il giornale**
journalist, newspaperman **il giornalista**
journalism **il giornalismo**
editor **il redattore**
editor-in-chief **il redattore capo**
city editor **il redattore di notizie locali**

reporter **il cronista**
sports **gli sport**
sportswriter **il cronista sportivo**
correspondent **il corrispondente**
publishing house **la casa editrice**
editorial **l'articolo di fondo**
story **l'articolo**
news **le notizie**
news item, event **la notizia**
advertising **la pubblicità**
criticism **la critica**
headline **la testata**
press **la stampa**
front page **la prima pagina**
proofreader **il correttore di bozze**
printer's error **l'errore dello stampatore**
envelope **la busta**

dispatch **il dispaccio**
society page(s) **la vita di società**
comics, comic strip **i fumetti**
magazine **la rivista**
copy boy **il fattorino**
telephone **il telefono**
teletype **il telescrivente**
typewriter **la macchina da scrivere**
photograph **la fotografia**
boss **il capo**
eyeshade **la visiera**
desk **la scrivania**
work **il lavoro**

present-day **attuale**
always **sempre**
never **mai**
worldwide **mondiale**
only **unico**

L'ufficio di redazione

Analisi del disegno

1. Che fa la donna?
2. Che fa l'uomo dalla visiera?
3. Chi sta telefonando?
4. Che fanno i due giornalisti in fondo a sinistra?
5. Dove ci sono alcune fotografie?
6. Dov'è, e che sta facendo il fattorino?
7. Come sa Lei che questo è un ufficio di redazione?
8. Descriva il disegno.

Punti di partenza

9. Chi è il capo dei cronisti?
10. Che fa il correttore di bozze?
11. Su che pagina di un giornale si trova la testata?
12. Chi scrive sulle notizie locali?
13. Quali sono alcune delle differenze fra un giornale ed una revista?
14. Chi redige le notizie sportive?
15. Qual è la differenza tra un cronista ed un corrispondente? Tra un cronista ed un redattore?
16. Che è un articolo di fondo?
17. Perchè sono indispensabili per un giornalista una macchina da scrivere ed un telefono?
18. Di quali sezioni si compone un giornale americano?
19. Quali sezioni di un giornale legge Lei e quali non legge? Perchè?
20. Legge Lei il giornale tutti i giorni? Se non lo legge, perchè no? Se lo legge, quale giornale è? Che pensa Lei di esso?

Temi per conversazione

1. Il giornalismo attuale negli Stati Uniti.
2. Descrizione di una notizia che nella stampa italiana sarebbe un articolo di prima pagina.
3. Perchè leggo sempre il giornale (o perchè non leggo mai il giornale).

to perform, act, or give a play **rappresentare**
to play a role **interpretare una parte**
to applaud **applaudire**
to raise **alzare**
to lower **abbassare**
to leave (*go away*) **andarsene**
to take place **aver luogo**
to find out about, to learn of **informarsi**
to tip **dare una mancia**
to stand, to be on one's feet **stare in piedi**
to marry, to get married **sposarsi (con), maritarsi (con)**
to forget **dimenticare**

theater **il teatro**
play **il dramma, l'opera teatrale**
playwright **il drammaturgo, il commediografo**
actor **l'attore**
actress **l'attrice**
audience **l'auditorio, il pubblico**

seat, location **il posto**
box seat **il palco**
orchestra seat **la poltrona di platea**
balcony seat **la galleria**
aisle **il corridoio**
row **la fila**
usher **la maschera**
ticket **il biglietto**
box office (ticket window) **la biglietteria**
lobby **il ridotto**
intermission **l'intermezzo, l'intervallo**
first performance, opening night **la prima**
stage **il palcoscenico**
curtain (*of a stage*) **il sipario**
act **l'atto**
scene **la scena**
(emergency) exit **l'uscita (di sicurezza)**
success **il buon esito, il successo**
failure **il fiasco**
gentleman **il signore**
beard **la barba**

glasses **gli occhiali**
wedding **lo sposalizio, il matrimonio, le nozze**
bride **la sposa novella, la sposa**
groom **lo sposo**
guest **l'ospite** (*m. & f.*),**l'invitato**
married couple **i coniugi, gli sposi**
newlywed **lo sposino, la sposina**
wedding ring **l'anello nuziale, la fede**
finger **il dito (le dita,** *pl.*)
hand **la mano (le mani,** *pl.*)
ring finger **l'anulare** (*m.*)
honeymoon **la luna di miele, il viaggio di nozze**
altar **l'altare** (*m.*)
pew **la panca (di chiesa)**
church **la chiesa**
temple (*Jewish*) **la sinagoga**
priest **il prete, il sacerdote**
rabbi **il rabbino**
Catholic **il cattolico**
Jew **l'ebreo, il giudeo**
Protestant **il protestante**
synopsis, summary **la sinossi**

Il teatro

Analisi del disegno

1. Chi non può vedere bene il palcoscenico? Perchè?
2. Dov'è il palco che si vede nel disegno?
3. Descriva il signore che se ne va.
4. Che scena stanno rappresentando nel dramma?
5. Quale parte sta interpretando ognuno degli attori sul palcoscenico?
6. Crede Lei che lo sposalizio abbia luogo in una chiesa cattolica o protestante o in una sinagoga? Perchè?
7. Dove c'è un'uscita di sicurezza in questo teatro?

Punti di partenza

8. Dove si comprano i biglietti per il teatro?
9. Quante classi di biglietti si possono comprare in un teatro e qual è il posto di ogni classe?
10. Che cosa deve fare la maschera?
11. In Italia si aspetta sempre che uno dia una mancia alla maschera. Che pensa Lei di quest'uso?
12. Quando si alza e quando si abbassa il sipario?
13. Dove si può andare durante l'intervallo?
14. Come s'informa un drammaturgo se la prima del suo dramma è stato un successo o un fiasco?
15. Nomini un'opera teatrale che Lei ha visto recentemente. Se non ne ha visto, perchè no?
16. Che è la luna di miele?
17. Su quale dito e di quale mano si mette la fede della sposa il giorno del suo sposalizio?
18. Che succederebbe se nel giorno dello sposalizio lo sposo dimenticasse la fede della sposa?
19. Quali sono alcuni dei problemi tipici degli sposini?
20. Ci descriva il suo sposalizio se Lei è sposato. Se non è sposato, dica perchè no.

Temi per conversazione

1. Perchè se ne va dal teatro il signore che sta in piedi nel corridoio.
2. Una sinossi dei tre atti del dramma che si vede in questo disegno.
3. Descrizione di un teatro e della prima di un dramma.

to play (*a musical instrument*) **suonare, sonare**
to conduct **dirigere**
to sing **cantare**
to improvise **improvvisare**
to point **puntare**
to make use of **servirsi di**
to use **adoperare**
to wear, to have on **indossare**
to take off, to remove **togliere**

symphony orchestra **l'orchestra sinfonica**
opera **l'opera**
symphony **la sinfonia**
musician **il musicista, il sonatore**
conductor **il direttore, il maestro**
composer **il compositore**
composition, (musical) piece **la composizione**
baton **la bacchetta**
theater **il teatro**
member (of the orchestra) **il professore d'orchestra**
(music) stand **il leggio**

note **la nota**
row **la fila**
tails (*formal wear*) **il frac**
melody **la melodia**
harmony **l'armonia**
rhythm **il ritmo**
motif, theme **il motivo, il tema**
movement **il movimento**
overture, prelude **il preludio**
fugue **la fuga**
piano **il pianoforte**
grand piano **il pianoforte a coda**
wind instrument **lo strumento a fiato**
flute **il flauto**
oboe **l'oboe** (*m.*)
bassoon **il fagotto**
horn **il corno**
trumpet **la tromba**
trombone **il trombone**
clarinet **il clarinetto**
tuba **la tuba**
stringed instrument **lo strumento a corda**

string, cord **la corda**
bow **l'arco, l'archetto**
violin **il violino**
viola **la viola**
violoncello **il violoncello**
harp **l'arpa**
lyre **la lira**
percussion instrument **lo strumento a percussione**
kettle drum **il timpano**
drumstick **la bacchetta**
finger **il dito (le dita,** *pl.***)**
cymbal **il cimbalo**
shoe **la scarpa**
life **la vita**
woman **la donna**

slow(ly), soft(ly) **adagio**
moderately slow(ly) **andante**
brisk, with cheer **allegro**
lively, with animation **vivace**
loud(ly), with power **forte**
by heart **a memoria**
while **mentre**

80

L'orchestra sinfonica

Analisi del disegno

1. Quanti professori d'orchestra possiamo vedere?
2. Quanti strumenti a fiato può identificare Lei e quali sono?
3. Dove sono gli strumenti a corda? A percussione?
4. Quali strumenti suonano le donne del disegno?
5. Che indossa il direttore?
6. Perchè punta il dito il direttore?
7. Chi ha tolto le scarpe?
8. Nomini un ritmo che il direttore d'orchestra potrebbe indicare con la sua bacchetta.
9. Come si servono del leggio i professori d'orchestra?

Punti di partenza

10. Cosa significa quando il maestro non ha leggio o non si serve del leggio?
11. Se Lei fosse musicista d'orchestra sinfonica, quale strumento vorrebbe suonare?
12. Con che si suona un violino? Un timpano?
13. In genere quanti movimenti ha una sinfonia?
14. Qual è la differenza tra un'opera ed una sinfonia?
15. Che cosa è il preludio di un'opera?
16. Nomini alcuni dei grandi compositori di sinfonie o di opere italiane.
17. Perchè è la musica sinfonica tecnicamente più complicata che la musica d'opera?
18. Secondo Lei, quali sono gli strumenti più importanti di un'orchestra sinfonica?
19. Quali strumenti d'orchestra sinfonica si possono adoperare anche per la musica jazz o popolare?
20. Che possono fare i musicisti di jazz mentre suonano che non possono fare i musicisti d'orchestra sinfonica?

Temi per conversazione

1. Il genere di musica che mi piace di più.
2. Lo strumento che so suonare.
3. La vita di uno dei musicisti della terza fila del disegno.

to work **lavorare**
to be self-employed **lavorare in proprio**
to earn **guadagnare**
to employ **impiegare**
to repair **riparare, aggiustare**
to saw **segare**
to build **costruire**
to deliver **consegnare, distribuire**
to sew **cucire**
to cut **tagliare**
to carve **tagliare, trinciare**
to cook **cucinare**
to stir **mescolare**
to wear, to have, to have on (oneself) **portare; avere su di sè**
to deduct **ritenere**
to be similar **somigliarsi**

work, job **il lavoro, l'impiego**
worker, wage earner **il lavoratore, l'operaio**
trade, craft **il mestiere**

profession **la professione**
employer **il datore di lavoro**
employee **l'impiegato**
working class **la classe operaia, la classe lavoratrice, il proletariato**
wages **la paga, il salario**
salary, stipend **lo stipendio**
overtime **il lavoro straordinario**
social security **la previdenza sociale**
withholding tax **la ritenuta (delle imposte)**
shoe **la scarpa**
shoemaker **il calzolaio**
carpenter **il falegname**
tool **l'utensile** (*m.*), **l'arnese** (*m.*)
saw **la sega**
board (*piece of lumber*) **la tavola (di legno)**
milk **il latte**
milkman **il lattaio**
tailor **il sarto**
cloth, fabric **la stoffa**

needle **l'ago**
thread **il filo**
button **il bottone**
meat **la carne**
butcher **il macellaio**
knife **il coltello**
cook **il cuoco**
food **il cibo, l'alimento**
ladle **il cucchiaione**
dipper **il mestolo**
pot **la pentola**
apron **il grembiale, il grembiule**
uniform **l'uniforme** (*f.*)
tie **la cravatta**
(suit) jacket **la giacca**
mailman, letter carrier **il postino**
explanation **la spiegazione**
instrument **lo strumento**

bald **calvo**
seldom **di rado**
almost **quasi**
left-handed **mancino**
besides **oltre a**
as well as **tanto . . . come**

I mestieri

Analisi del disegno

1. Chi sono calvi, o quasi calvi?
2. Con che arnesi sta lavorando il falegname? Che sta facendo?
3. Che cosa porta il lattaio nella mano e che sta facendo?
4. Che sta cucendo il sarto? Che oggetti del suo mestiere si vedono?
5. Che tiene il macellaio nella mano e che sta facendo?
6. Descriva il cuoco e ciò che sta facendo.
7. Quali degli uomini portano un grembiale? Quale porta un'uniforme? Quale porta una cravatta?
8. Come sappiamo che il falegname, il sarto ed il macellaio non sono mancini?
9. Quali usano la mano destra oltre al falegname, il sarto ed il macellaio?
10. Quali di questi uomini lavorano in proprio e quali sono impiegati?

Punti di partenza

11. Quale dei lavori dei sei uomini preferirebbe Lei? Perchè?
12. Che è un falegname?
13. In che si somiglia un lattaio e un postino?
14. Quali sono le differenze e le somiglianze tra un macellaio ed un cuoco?
15. Il calzolaio negli Stati Uniti fa di rado le scarpe. Che cosa fa?
16. Che cosa vuol dire « proletariato »?
17. Spieghi la differenza tra « paga » e « stipendio ».
18. Che si ritiene dalla paga di un lavoratore e dallo stipendio di un professore, e perchè?
19. Che è il lavoro straordinario?
20. Qual è la differenza fra un mestiere ed una professione?

Temi per conversazione

1. Come cucinare . . . .
2. Una spiegazione della previdenza sociale e la ritenuta delle imposte.
3. La vita del lattaio (o di uno degli altri cinque uomini del disegno).

to build **costruire**

to assemble, to put together
  montare

to repair, to mend **riparare**

to hammer **martellare**

to saw **segare**

to screw **avvitare**

to chop **fendere**

to hold **tenere**

to fasten **afferrare, fissare**

to hang **appendere**

to drill (*a hole*) **forare**

to cut **tagliare**

to contain **contenere**

to appear **apparire**

to be necessary **bisognare**

handyman, artisan (*in own
  house*) **l'artigiano « di casa
  propria »**

hobby **il passatempo, il hobby**

carpenter's workbench **il banco
  da falegname**

structure, frame **la costruzione,
  la struttura**

tool **l'utensile** (*m.*), **l'arnese**
  (*m.*)

hardware store **il negozio di fer-
  ramenta**

vise **la morsa**

screw **la vite**

hammer **il martello**

saw **la sega**

hacksaw **il seghetto per i me-
  talli**

screwdriver **il cacciavite**

nail **il chiodo**

plane **la pialla**

monkey wrench **la chiave inglese**

pliers **le tenaglie, la pinza**

hatchet **l'accetta**

shears **le cesoie**

wire **il filo metallico**

chisel **lo scalpello**

level **la livella**

brace **il trapano a mano, la
  menarola**

bit **la punta**

crowbar **la leva di ferro**

sandpaper **la cartavetrata**

T square **la riga a T**

oilcan **l'oliatore** (*m.*)

(*glass*) jar **il vaso (di vetro)**

wood (*lumber*) **il legno**

hardwood **il legno duro**

softwood **il legno dolce**

oak **la quercia**

pine **il pino**

shaving (*of wood*) **il truciolo**

cabinet **l'armadietto**

glue **la colla**

size **la grandezza**

piece **il pezzo**

hole **il buco, il foro**

use **l'uso**

useful **utile**

at first, as the first step **per prima**

finally, as the last step **per ultimo**

different **distinto**

similar **simile**

easy **facile**

also **pure**

L'artigiano di casa propria

Analisi del disegno

1. Che sta costruendo l'artigiano « di casa propria » ?
2. Che contengono i vasi di vetro?
3. Nomini gli oggetti sopra il banco da falegname.
4. Quali utensili son appesi nell'armadietto?
5. Quale delle seghe si usa per tagliare il filo metallico? Quale altro utensile pure taglia il filo metallico?
6. Esiste un arnese molto utile per costruire che non appare nel disegno. Qual è quest'arnese?
7. Quale di queste cose crede Lei che si usi per prima, e quale per ultimo, nel costruire il modello che è sopra il banco da falegname: la pialla, la sega, la cartavetrata?
8. Quali utensili crede Lei che non servano per montare il modello che sta costruendo l'uomo?
9. Come sappiamo che l'uomo ha usato o lo scalpello o la pialla?

Punti di partenza

10. Che specie di legno è più facile da segare?
11. Per che cosa si usa l'accetta?
12. Che cosa è il truciolo? Quali utensili producono trucioli?
13. Che è un artigiano « di casa propria » ?
14. Per che cosa si usa una morsa?
15. Che arnese si usa per martellare?
16. Perchè si usano il trapano a mano e le punte? Perchè ci sono distinte grandezze di punte?
17. Quale utensile si usa per avvitare?
18. Nomini un legno duro; nomini un legno dolce.
19. Quale utensile bisogna tenere con le due mani?
20. In che maniera simile si possono usare la chiave inglese, le tenaglie e la morsa? Lo scalpello e la pialla? Il martello e l'accetta?

Temi per conversazione

1. Come costruire . . . .
2. Distinti tipi di utensili ed i loro usi.
3. Il mio hobby preferito.

to make the bed **fare il letto**
to clean **pulire**
to wash **lavare**
to dry **asciugare**
to scrub **strofinare**
to sweep **scopare**
to iron **stirare**
to make the meal **preparare il pasto**
to accomplish **eseguire**
to dissolve **sciogliere, dissolvere**
to protect **proteggere**
to be broken, not to work **non funzionare, essere rotto**

domestic chore or task **il lavoro domestico**
housework **i lavori domestici**
household **la casa, il focolare**
housewife **la casalinga, la massaia**
servant, maid **la cameriera, la domestica**

bed **il letto**
sheet **il lenzuolo**
mattress **il materasso, la materassa**
bedspread **la coperta da letto**
pillow **il guanciale**
pillowcase **la federa**
blanket **la coperta**
rug **il tappeto**
vacuum cleaner **l'aspirapolvere** (*m.*)
dish **il piatto**
dish rack **lo scolapiatti**
pot **la pentola**
saucepan **la casseruola**
frying pan **la padella**
handle **il manico**
sink **l'acquaio, il lavandino**
soap **il sapone**
detergent **il detersivo**
grease **il grasso**
automatic dishwasher **il lavastoviglie automatico**

garbage disposer **la macinaimmondizie, la tritarifiuti**
glove **il guanto**
floor **il pavimento**
bucket **il secchio**
scrubbing brush **la spazzola dura**
broom **la scopa**
dustpan **la paletta per la spazzatura**
stool **lo sgabello**
trash can, garbage can **il bidone dei rifiuti, il porta-immondizie**
sofa, couch **il divano, il sofà**
hand **la mano (le mani,** *pl.***)**

dirty **sporco, sudicio**
clean **pulito**
tired **stanco**
at home **a casa, in casa**
as soon as **appena**
then **poi**

I lavori domestici

Analisi del disegno

1. Quali di questi lavori domestici si devono fare tutti i giorni?
2. Dove vede Lei guanciali con federe?
3. Quali di questi lavori si possono eseguire rapidamente?
4. Per quali due lavori si potrebbe usare guanti e perchè?
5. Perchè stanno i piatti nello scolapiatti?
6. Che sta lavando nell'acquaio il signore?
7. Se c'è una macinaimmondizie in una di queste scene, perchè non si può vedere?
8. Che c'è dentro il secchio?
9. Dov'è la paletta per la spazzatura?
10. Chi sta usando il sapone o il detersivo?
11. Dove c'è un bidone dei rifiuti?

Punti di partenza

12. Per che cosa si usa il detersivo?
13. Quando si usa un aspirapolvere e quando una spazzola?
14. Per che cosa si usa una scopa?
15. Descriva la differenza tra una pentola, una casseruola ed una padella.
16. Per quale lavoro domestico preferirebbe Lei avere una cameriera, e perchè?
17. Dove si mettono i piatti ad asciugare appena lavati?
18. Che si mette sopra la coperta facendo il letto?
19. Che si mette tra il materasso e la coperta?
20. Lei è casalinga senza domestica. Lei è stanca. I piatti non sono lavati (il lavastoviglie automatico non funziona), il pavimento è sporco, i letti non sono fatti ed i bambini staranno in casa tutto il giorno. Che fa Lei poi?

Temi per conversazione

1. Come fare un letto.
2. I lavori domestici sono interminabili.
3. Alcune differenze tra i lavori domestici in Italia e negli Stati Uniti.

to work **lavorare**	farm **la fattoria, il podere**	fence **il recinto**
to dig **scavare**	horse **il cavallo**	wall **il muro**
to cultivate **coltivare**	cow **la vacca**	gate **il cancello, la porta**
to plant **piantare**	grain **il grano**	post **il palo**
to feed **dare da mangiare (a)**	barn **il granaio**	tool, implement **l'attrezzo**
to store **immagazzinare**	stable **la scuderia, la stalla**	rake **il rastrello**
to graze **pascolare**	sheep **la pecora**	hoe **la zappa**
to lead, to drive **guidare**	duck **l'anitra**	shovel **la pala**
to hang up clothes **appendere i vestiti**	goose **l'oca**	stake **il palo, lo steccone**
	pond **lo stagno**	garden **il giardino**
to get along well **andare bene d'accordo**	donkey **l'asino, il somaro**	tree **l'albero**
	dog **il cane**	vegetable **il legume**
to suggest **suggerire**	hen **la gallina**	farmer **il contadino**
to lean **appoggiar(si)**	chicken **il pollo**	wife **la moglie**
to bark **abbaiare**	turkey **il tacchino**	son **il figlio**
to open **aprire**	cat **il gatto**	daughter **la figlia**
to help **aiutare**	field **il campo**	vacation **la vacanza, le vacanze**
	tractor **il trattore**	
		only **unico**

La vita alla fattoria

Analisi del disegno

1. Quali sono i lavori del contadino in una fattoria come questa? I lavori della moglie del contadino? Dei suoi figli?
2. Dove sono le anitre e le oche?
3. Che sta facendo l'unica vacca?
4. Chi conduce il trattore?
5. Dove sono i recinti e i muri?
6. Dov'è il gatto e che sta facendo?
7. Quali attrezzi si possono vedere e dove sono?
8. Dove hanno piantato legumi?
9. Per che cosa son stati usati gli attrezzi?
10. Che fa il figlio del contadino?
11. Perchè abbaia il cane?
12. Che sta facendo la moglie del contadino?
13. Dove sono le galline e dove sono i tacchini?
14. Per che cosa servono gli stecconi che sono nel giardino?
15. Le pare che questa fattoria sia grande o piccola? Perchè?
16. Che c'è in questo disegno che ci suggerisce che questa sia una fattoria europea?
17. Dove andrebbero questi animali se i due cancelli fossero aperti?
18. Che cosa potrebbe dire il cavallo alla pecora?

Punti di partenza

19. Qual è la differenza tra un granaio ed una scuderia?
20. Quali animali di fattoria vanno bene d'accordo generalmente e quali no?

Temi per conversazione

1. Vantaggi e svantaggi del vivere in una fattoria.
2. Descrizione di una grande fattoria.
3. Perchè (non) mi piacerebbe passare le vacanze in una fattoria.

to drive **guidare, condurre**	street **la strada**	church **la chiesa**
to stop **fermare**	block (*of buildings or houses*)	awning **la tenda**
to push **spingere**	**l'isolato urbano, il blocco di**	bench **la panca**
to obey, to respect **rispettare**	**fabbricati**	fountain **la fontana**
to watch (over) **vigilare (su)**	downtown **il centro**	sidewalk **il marciapiede**
to indicate **indicare**	traffic light **il semaforo**	tree **l'albero**
to live, to dwell **vivere, abitare**	vehicle **il veicolo**	flower **il fiore**
to injure **ferire**	automobile **l'automobile** (*f.*), **la**	leaf **la foglia**
to tell, to relate **raccontare**	**macchina**	grass **l'erba**
to sit down **sedersi**	bicycle **la bicicletta**	gutter **la cunetta**
to read **leggere**	motorcycle **la motocicletta**	pigeon **il piccione**
to show, to demonstrate **mos-**	baby carriage **la carrozzina per**	England **Inghilterra**
trare, dimostrare	**bambini**	
to feed **dare da mangiare (a)**	motor **il motore**	red **rosso**
to try (to) **cercare (di)**	policeman **l'agente** (*m.*) **di po-**	yellow **giallo**
	lizia, il poliziotto	green **verde**
main square **la piazza principale**	traffic accident **l'incidente** (*m.*)	white **bianco**
small square, little park **la piaz-**	**stradale**	black **nero**
zetta	helmet **il casco**	in color **a colori**
city **la città**	store **il negozio**	either one **qualsiasi**
town **la cittadina, il paese**	theater **il teatro**	

La piazza principale

Analisi del disegno

1. Che sta facendo l'agente di polizia?
2. Chi porta un casco e perchè?
3. Descriva ciò che vede nel blocco di fabbricati dietro la piazzetta.
4. Come sa Lei che questo disegno non rappresenta una scena in Inghilterra?
5. Spieghi perchè questa scena potrebbe essere (1) europea o (2) americana o (3) qualsiasi delle due.
6. Dov'è la carrozzina e chi la spinge?
7. Chi sta cercando di dare da mangiare al piccione?
8. Descriva la piazzetta.
9. Come sa Lei che è di giorno e non di notte?
10. Chi sta leggendo e dove?
11. Perchè è venuto al centro l'uomo seduto sul banco?
12. Quali sarebbero i colori di alcune delle cose che vediamo qui se questo disegno fosse a colori?
13. Quanti tipi di veicoli vede Lei nel disegno e quali sono?
14. Perchè è possibile che ci siano (o che non ci siano) foglie dentro la fontana?

Punti di partenza

15. Quali sono i colori di un semaforo e che cosa ci indica ogni colore?
16. Perchè deve uno rispettare i semafori?
17. Quali sono le differenze tra una bicicletta ed una motocicletta?
18. Che cos'è e dov'è la cunetta?
19. Preferisce Lei vivere in una città o in un paese? Perchè?
20. Descriva il centro della città (o paese) dove abita Lei ora.

Temi per conversazione

1. Ciò che mi raccontò l'uomo che sta seduto sulla panca.
2. La mia piazza principale favorita.
3. Main Street, U.S.A.

to catch fire **incendiarsi**
to burn (up, down) **bruciare**
to start a fire **accendere**
to put out a fire **spegnere**
to asphyxiate **asfissiare**
to faint **svenire**
to rescue **salvare, soccorrere**
to destroy **distruggere**
to connect **attaccare**
to notify, to summon **avvisare**
to protect **proteggere**
to shout **gridare**
to escape **scappar(si), sfuggir(si)**
to jump **saltare**
to injure **ferire**
to take, to transport **prendere, portare**
to get, to obtain **ottenere**
to photograph **fotografare**
to show **dimostrare**

fire **il fuoco, l'incendio**
fireman **il pompiere, il vigile del fuoco**
fire department **il corpo di pompieri**
fire house **la caserma dei pompieri**
fire engine **l'autopompa**
fire extinguisher **l'estintore** (*m.*)
firebug **il piromante, l'incendiario**
fire alarm box **la cassetta per il segnale d'allarme**
alarm **l'allarme** (*m.*)
hydrant **l'idrante** (*m.*)
smoke **il fumo**
flame **la fiamma**
hose **il tubo da getto**

ladder **la scala a pioli**
helmet **l'elmo (da pompiere)**
building **l'edificio, il fabbricato**
roof **il tetto**
emergency exit **l'uscita di sicurezza**
siren **la sirena**
ambulance **l'ambulanza**
hospital **l'ospedale** (*m.*)
equipment **l'equipaggiamento**
coat **la giacca, il soprabito**
arm **il braccio (le braccia, *pl.*)**
water **l'acqua**
photographer **il fotografo**

Help! **Aiuto!**
fireproof **incombustibile**
brave **coraggioso**
each, every **ogni**

Fuoco!

Analisi del disegno

1. Che sarà accaduto alla ragazza che è nelle braccia del pompiere?
2. Che starà gridando il pompiere che è in primo piano?
3. Che sta facendo il fotografo?
4. Descriva ciò che sta accadendo dentro l'autopompa.
5. Perchè crede Lei che quest'incendio distruggerà (o che non distruggerà) l'edificio?
6. Che farebbe Lei se fosse sul tetto dell'edificio che sta bruciando?

Punti di partenza

7. Come può dimostrare un pompiere che è coraggioso?
8. A che attacca il pompiere la manica dell'autopompa per ottenere acqua?
9. Come si può avvisare i pompieri in caso d'incendio?
10. Perchè portano gli elmi i pompieri?
11. Che è una caserma dei pompieri?
12. Perchè usano i pompieri una scala?
13. Per che cosa si usa un'ambulanza?
14. Come si scapperebbe Lei dal fabbricato dove si trova in caso d'incendio?
15. Spieghi: « Dove c'è fumo c'è fuoco ».
16. Che equipaggiamento ha ogni autopompa?
17. Che è un piromante?
18. Che significa un incendio di tre segnali d'allarme?
19. Che è una giacca incombustibile?
20. Come si può spegnere un piccolo incendio?

Temi per conversazione

1. Il giorno che vidi un incendio.
2. Ciò che fanno in una caserma dei pompieri quando non ci sono incendi.
3. Il grande incendio di Chicago dell'anno 1871.

to take a picture **prendere una fotografia**
to climb **arrampicarsi su**
to raise, to lift **alzare, levare**
to feed **dar da mangiare a**
to protect **proteggere**
to escape **scappar(si), sfuggir(si)**
to eat **mangiare**
to drink **bere**
to visit **visitare**
to sit **sedersi**

zoo **il giardino zoologico, lo zoo**
cage **la gabbia**
house (*for animals*) **la casetta**
animal **l'animale** (*m.*)
beast **la bestia**

king **il re**
monkey **la scimmia**
bear **l'orso**
lion **il leone**
tiger **la (il) tigre**
elephant **l'elefante** (*m.*)
gorilla **la gorilla**
giraffe **la giraffa**
wolf **il lupo**
deer **il cervo**
fox **la volpe**
camel **il cammello**
leopard **il leopardo**
panther **la pantera**
zebra **la zebra**
hippopotamus **l'ippopotamo**
rhinoceros **il rinoceronte**
alligator **l'alligatore** (*m.*)

snake **il serpente**
reptile **il rettile**
human being **l'essere umano**
balloon **il palloncino**
camera **la macchina fotografica**
railing **la ringhiera**
(drinking) fountain **la fontana (pubblica)**
bench **la panca**
sign, notice **l'avviso**
ditch **il fossato**
hill **la collina**
banana **la banana**
banana peel **la buccia di banana**
meat **la carne**
custom **il costume**

wild **selvatico, feroce**
around **intorno (a)**

Il giardino zoologico

Analisi del disegno

1. Dov'è la scimmia e che sta facendo?
2. Che ha mangiato la scimmia? Come lo sa?
3. Chi tiene una macchina fotografica e che sta facendo?
4. Chi tiene un palloncino e dov'è?
5. Perchè il padre sta alzando suo figlio?
6. Dove sta seduta la persona?
7. Quali animali non sono nelle gabbie? Perchè sono necessarie le gabbie?
8. Nomini alcuni animali che non sono in questo disegno.
9. Dove crede Lei che ci sia un fossato?
10. Quale animale crede Lei che viva nella casetta sulla collina?
11. Con chi crede Lei che stia parlando il ragazzino che sta in primo piano? Che può stare dicendo?

Punti di partenza

12. Chi è il « re delle bestie »?
13. Quali animali mangiano carne e quali no?
14. Che avviso si vede generalmente in un giardino zoologico?
15. Descriva uno zoo che Lei ha visitato.
16. Descriva la somiglianza fra l'essere umano e la scimmia.
17. Perchè c'è una ringhiera intorno a molte delle gabbie?
18. Che farebbe Lei se fosse in un giardino zoologico dove un lupo s'era sfuggito dalla sua gabbia?
19. Che disse la giraffa alla gorilla?
20. Nomini alcuni animali che possiamo vedere senza visitare lo zoo.

Temi per conversazione

1. Non tutte le scimmie si trovano in giardini zoologici.
2. L'interessante della giraffa.
3. Una giornata al giardino zoologico.

to be (*weather*) **fare (tempo, freddo, caldo)**	weather **il tempo**	degree **il grado**
to be (*body temperature*) **avere (freddo, caldo)**	climate **il clima**	zero **lo zero**
to forecast **prevedere**	season **la stagione (dell'anno)**	seed **la seme**
to rain **piovere**	spring **la primavera**	leaf **la foglia**
to snow **nevicare**	summer **l'estate** (*f.*)	tulip **il tulipano**
to melt **sciogliere**	fall **l'autunno**	bird **l'uccello**
to freeze **gelar(si), agghiacciar(si)**	winter **l'inverno**	rake **il rastrello**
to plant **piantare**	freezing point **il punto di congelamento**	hoe **la zappa**
to dig **scavare**	water **l'acqua**	trench **il solco**
to bloom **fiorire**	rain **la pioggia**	face **la faccia (le facce**, *pl.*)
to sing **cantare**	raindrop **la goccia di pioggia**	ice cream **il gelato**
to dry (off), to wipe (off) **asciugar(si)**	snow **la neve**	
to rake **rastrellare**	snowball **la palla di neve**	cloudy **nuvoloso**
to throw **gettare, lanciare**	ice **il ghiaccio**	dry **secco**
to rise (*of temperature*) **aumentare**	sun **il sole**	damp, humid **umido**
to indicate, to tell **indicare**	cloud **la nuvola**	tomorrow **domani**
to have just **avere appena** + *participio passato*	wind **il vento**	besides **oltre (a)**
to fall (down) **cadere**	hail **la grandine**	32° Fahrenheit = 0° centigrado.

storm **la tempesta, il temporale**
thunder **il tuono**
lightning **il lampo, il fulmine**
tornado **il ciclone, il tornado**
hurricane **l'uragano**

Per convertire gradi centigradi in gradi Fahrenheit, moltiplichi per 9, divida per 5 e aggiunga 32. Per convertire gradi Fahrenheit in centigradi, ne sottragga 32, moltiplichi per 5 e divida per 9.

Il tempo

Analisi del disegno

1. Oltre all'uccello che canta (nel primo disegno a sinistra), quali altre cose ci indicano che è primavera?
2. Che fa l'uomo con la zappa?
3. Che fa la signora nello stesso disegno?
4. Chi ha appena comprato un gelato?
5. Perchè si asciuga la faccia il signore?
6. Quale dei disegni indica che è autunno e perchè?
7. Che stanno facendo i ragazzi nella neve?

Punti di partenza

8. Qual è il punto di congelamento dell'acqua?
9. Che è la neve? Che è il ghiaccio?
10. In quale stagione dell'anno fioriscono i tulipani?
11. Come si sa quando piantare semi?
12. Descriva il clima della regione dove si trova Lei adesso.
13. Perchè non può piovere quando c'è sole?
14. Quando si scioglie la neve?
15. Quale sarebbe l'equivalente in centigradi quando la temperatura aumenta fino a 95° Fahrenheit?
16. Quanti gradi Fahrenheit corrispondono a 25° centigradi di temperatura?
17. Qual è la temperatura in Fahrenheit e quale in centigradi dove Lei si trova in questo momento?
18. Descriva il tempo che fa oggi.
19. Preveda il tempo di domani.
20. Descriva le differenze tra l'estate e l'inverno.

Temi per conversazione

1. La stagione dell'anno che mi piace di più.
2. I tipi di tempeste.
3. I vari climi degli Stati Uniti.

to irrigate **irrigare**
to flow **scorrere, fluire**
to control **governare**
to row **remare**
to steer **guidare**
to float **galleggiare, stare a galla**
to drink **bere**
to swim **nuotare**
to render, to make **rendere**

water **l'acqua**
fresh water **l'acqua dolce**
salt water **l'acqua salata, l'acqua di mare**
sea **il mare**
ocean **l'oceano**
tide **la marea**
seasickness **il mal di mare**
high tide **l'alta marea**
low tide **la bassa marea**
current, flow **la corrente, il**

corso
wave **l'onda**
shore **la costa**
river **il fiume**
bay **la baia**
inlet **l'estuario**
lake **il lago**
stream, brook **la corrente, il ruscello**
waterfall **la cascata**
canal **il canale**
irrigation ditch **il canale per l'irrigazione**
spring **la sorgente**
swamp **il pantano, la palude**
well **il pozzo**
dam **la diga**
rain **la pioggia**
fisherman **il pescatore**
ship **la nave**
sailboat **la barca a vela**

barge **la chiatta**
rowboat **la barca a remi**
oar **il remo**
rudder **il timone**
land **la terra**
mountain **la montagna, il monte**
desert **il deserto**
oasis **l'oasi** (f.)
origin **l'origine** (f.)
room (*space*) **lo spazio**
usefulness **l'utilità**

deep **profondo**
shallow **poco profondo**
rough (*not calm*) **agitato**
calm **calmo, placido**
clean **pulito**
dirty **sporco**
salt(y) **salato**
only **unico**
each one **ognuno**

Le acque

Analisi del disegno

1. Quale dei sei disegni crede Lei che sia l'unico le cui acque hanno maree?
2. Nomini una o due differenze tra l'aspetto e la composizione dell'acqua del mare e dell'acqua della cascata.
3. Dove vede Lei una barca a vela e perchè questa non si potrebbe trovare in nessuno degli altri disegni?
4. Di che origine crede Lei che possa essere l'acqua del lago?
5. Come si guida la chiatta?
6. Descriva la scena del fiume.
7. In quale dei disegni crede Lei che l'acqua sia più profonda ed in quale poco profonda?
8. Che sta facendo ognuno delle persone visibili?

Punti di partenza

9. Quali condizioni possono produrre il mal di mare?
10. Quale marea preferiscono i pescatori che pescano in acqua salata?
11. Che cosa è un deserto?
12. Che cosa è un'oasi?
13. Spieghi la differenza tra un lago ed un fiume e tra un ruscello ed un fiume.
14. In quale lago dello stato di Utah è facile galleggiare?
15. Che cosa rende famose le Cascate del Niagara?
16. Descriva l'acqua di un pantano.
17. Perchè servono un canale ed un canale per l'irrigazione?
18. Spieghi la relazione tra « costa » e « baia ».
19. Perchè non si può nuotare in una sorgente?
20. Che genere di acqua preferisce Lei per nuotare? Perchè?

Temi per conversazione

1. I fiumi navigabili d'Italia.
2. L'utilità delle dighe.
3. La conservazione dell'acqua.

to border (on) **confinare (con)**
to cross, to go through **attraversare**
to constitute **costituire**

map **la carta geografica**
topographical map **la carta fisica, la carta topografica**
border **il confine, la frontiera**
location **la situazione, la posizione**
boot **lo stivale**
north **il nord**
Northern Italy **l'Italia settentrionale**
south **il sud**
Southern Italy **l'Italia meridionale**
south (*of Italy*) **il Mezzogiorno**
west **l'ovest** (*m.*)
east **l'est** (*m.*)

middle **il mezzo**
Alps **le Alpi**
Vatican City **la Città del Vaticano**
peninsula **la penisola**
island **l'isola**
mountain **la montagna, il monte**
lake **il lago**
sea **il mare**
gulf **il golfo**
bay **la baia**
coast **la costa**
canal **il canale**
river **il fiume**
sources (*of a river*) **le sorgenti**
(mountain) chain **la catena**
volcano **il vulcano**
backbone **la spina dorsale**
city **la città**
province **la provincia**

country (*nation*) **il paese, la nazione**
republic **la repubblica**
monarchy **la monarchia**
democracy **la democrazia**
dictatorship **la dittatura**
dictator **il dittatore**
constitution **la costituzione**
government **il governo**
parliament **il parlamento**
senate **il senato**
chamber of deputies (*lower house of parliament*) **la camera dei deputati**
church **la chiesa**
pope **il papa**
The Holy See **La Santa Sede**
chief, head, leader **il capo, il duce**

Catholic **catolico**
today, nowadays **oggi**

La carta d'Italia

Analisi del disegno

1. Che forma ha l'Italia? Che configurazione topografica ha?
2. Sulla carta geografica d'Europa, dove si trova l'Italia?
3. Che paesi consinano con l'Italia? .
4. Nomini due province italiane e descriva dove si trovano.
5. In quali province si trovano le città di Roma, Napoli, Bari, Firenze, Bologna, Venezia, Milano, Genova e Torino?
6. Nomini l'isola italiana più grande. Dove si trova?
7. Descriva la posizione geografica di Palermo e di Cagliari.
8. Quali sono i piccoli mari che costituiscono il Mare Mediterraneo?
9. Dove sono le sorgenti del fiume Po? Del fiume Adige?
10. Come si chiama il fiume che attraversa Roma? Firenze?
11. Ci sono tre laghi nell'Italia settentrionale e due piccolissime isole nell'Italia meridionale che molti turisti visitano. Quali sono?
12. Quale catena di montagne si chiama « la spina dorsale » d'Italia? Perchè?
13. Che sono il Monte Vesuvio ed il Monte Etna? Descriva le loro posizioni geografiche.
14. Quale città crede Lei che sia la più grande del Mezzogiorno?

Punti di partenza

15. In che altre nazioni c'è gente che parla l'italiano?
16. Perchè i turisti vogliono visitare Venezia?
17. Chi è il papa? Dov'è La Santa Sede?
18. Chi era Benito Mussolini? Che forma di governo c'era in Italia nella sua epoca?
19. Che forma di governo ha l'Italia oggi?
20. Che forma di governo preferisce Lei? Perchè?

Temi per conversazione

1. Luoghi interessanti d'Italia.
2. Perchè Roma è famosa.
3. Il governo d'Italia.

to explore **esplorare**
to travel **viaggiare**
to shine **risplendere, brillare**
to twinkle **scintillare**
to reflect **riflettere**
to revolve (about) **girare (intorno a)**
to rotate on, upon **ruotare (intorno a)**
to help **aiutare**
to recognize **riconoscere**
to comprehend **comprendere**
to pass **passare**
to memorize **imparare a memoria**

firmament **il firmamento**
universe **l'universo**
heaven(s) **il cielo**
solar system **il sistema solare**
outer space **lo spazio oltre-terrestre, lo spazio cosmico**
sun **il sole**

moon **la luna**
star **la stella**
constellation **la costellazione**
planet **il pianeta**
eclipse **l'eclissi** (*f.*)
nebula, nebulous **la nebulosa**
atmosphere **l'atmosfera**
Milky Way **la Via Lattea**
Big Dipper, Ursa Major **l'Orsa Maggiore**
Mercury **Mercurio**
Venus **Venere**
earth **Terra, la terra**
Mars **Marte**
Jupiter **Giove**
Saturn **Saturno**
Uranus **Urano**
Neptune **Nettuno**
Pluto **Plutone**
infinity **l'infinito, l'infinità**
distance **la distanza**
light-year **l'anno luce**
movement **il movimento**

shadow **l'ombra**
ring **l'anello**
axis **l'asse** (*m.*)
rocket **il razzo**
capsule **la capsula**
guided missile **il razzo tele-comandato, il missile tele-guidato**
atomic bomb **la bomba atomica**
force **la forza**
astronaut **l'astronauta** (*m.*)
group **il gruppo**
order **l'ordine** (*m.*)
purpose, aim **il proposito, lo scopo**
end **la fine**

simplified **semplificato**
if so **se sì, in caso affermativo**
if not **se no, al contrario**
where do we go from here? **dove andiamo a finire?**

Il firmamento

Analisi del disegno

1. Quale costellazione si vede in uno dei disegni?
2. Nel disegno della Terra, che oggetto si vede nello spazio oltre-terrestre?
3. Quale pianeta si vede in uno dei disegni? Come si riconosce?
4. Che si vede negli altri tre disegni?

Punti di partenza

5. In inglese si possono imparare a memoria i nove pianeti e il loro ordine di distanza dal sole per la prima lettera di ogni parola di questa frase: Mary's Vivacious Eyes Made John Sit Up Nights Pining. Inventi una frase di nove parole in italiano con lo stesso proposito.
6. Che è un'eclissi di luna?
7. Che è il sistema solare?
8. Che è una costellazione?
9. Qual è la differenza tra la luce di un pianeta e quella di una stella?
10. Crede Lei che Marte sarà esplorato da uomini della Terra? In caso affermativo, quando? Al contrario, perchè no?
11. Che è un astronauta?
12. Come può viaggiare un astronauta dalla Terra allo spazio oltre-terrestre?
13. Che cosa è un anno luce?
14. La Terra gira intorno al sole e ruota intorno al suo asse. Spieghi il movimento della luna.
15. Come ci aiuta la forza atomica a comprendere il sole?
16. Qual è il pianeta più grande? Il più piccolo?
17. Perchè non potrebbe vivere una persona della Terra sulla luna?
18. Che è la Via Lattea?
19. Quante stelle ci sono nel cielo?
20. Perchè è tanto difficile comprendere l'infinito?

Temi per conversazione

1. I pianeti del nostro sistema solare.
2. Una descrizione semplificata dell'universo.
3. Dove andiamo a finire?

Appendice

AUXILIARY VERBS (VERBI AUSILIARI)

INFINITIVE (INFINITO)

avere *to have*
essere *to be*

PERFECT INFINITIVE (INFINITO PERFETTO)

avere avuto *having had*
essendo stato *having been*

PRESENT PARTICIPLE (GERUNDIO)

avendo *having*
essendo *being, having*

PAST PARTICIPLE (PARTICIPIO PASSATO)

avuto *had*
stato *been*

SIMPLE TENSES (TEMPI SEMPLICI)

INDICATIVE MOOD (MODO INDICATIVO)

PRESENT (PRESENTE)

I have, do have	*I am*
ho	**sono**
hai	**sei**
ha	**è**
abbiamo	**siamo**
avete	**siete**
hanno	**sono**

IMPERFECT (IMPERFETTO)

I had, was having, *used to have*	*I was,* *used to be*
avevo	**ero**
avevi	**eri**
aveva	**era**
avevamo	**eravamo**
avevate	**eravate**
avevano	**erano**

PAST DEFINITE OR PAST ABSOLUTE (PASSATO REMOTO)

I had, did have	*I was*
ebbi	**fui**
avesti	**fosti**
ebbe	**fu**
avemmo	**fummo**

aveste	foste
ebbero	furono

FUTURE (FUTURO)

I will have	*I will be*
avrò	sarò
avrai	sarai
avrà	sarà
avremo	saremo
avrete	sarete
avranno	saranno

CONDITIONAL (CONDIZIONALE PRESENTE)

I would have	*I would be*
avrei	sarei
avresti	saresti
avrebbe	sarebbe
avremmo	saremmo
avreste	sareste
avrebbero	sarebbero

IMPERATIVE (IMPERATIVO)

have	*be*
abbi	sii
abbia	sia
abbiamo	siamo
abbiate	siate
abbiano	siano

SUBJUNCTIVE MOOD (MODO CONGIUNTIVO *OR* SOGGIUNTIVO)

PRESENT (PRESENTE)

(that) I may have	*(that) I may be*
abbia	sia
abbia	sia
abbia	sia
abbiamo	siamo
abbiate	siate
abbiano	siano

IMPERFECT (IMPERFETTO)

(that) I might (would) have	*(that) I might (would) be*
avessi	fossi
avessi	fossi
avesse	fosse
avessimo	fossimo

aveste   foste
avessero   fossero

COMPOUND TENSES (TEMPI COMPOSTI)

INDICATIVE MOOD (MODO INDICATIVO)

PRESENT PERFECT (PASSATO PROSSIMO)

I have had   *I have been*

ho ⎫   sono ⎫
hai ⎬ avuto   sei ⎬ stato(a)
ha ⎭   è ⎭

abbiamo ⎫   siamo ⎫
avete ⎬ avuto   siete ⎬ stati(e)
hanno ⎭   sono ⎭

PLUPERFECT (TRAPASSATO PROSSIMO)

I had had   *I had been*

avevo ⎫   ero ⎫
avevi ⎬ avuto   eri ⎬ stato(a)
aveva ⎭   era ⎭

avevamo ⎫   eravamo ⎫
avevate ⎬ avuto   eravate ⎬ stati(e)
avevano ⎭   erano ⎭

SECOND PLUPERFECT (TRAPASSATO REMOTO)

I had had   *I had been*

ebbi ⎫   fui ⎫
avesti ⎬ avuto   fosti ⎬ stato(a)
ebbe ⎭   fu ⎭

avemmo ⎫   fummo ⎫
aveste ⎬ avuto   foste ⎬ stati(e)
ebbero ⎭   furono ⎭

FUTURE PERFECT (FUTURO ANTERIORE)

I will have had   *I will have been*

avrò ⎫   sarò ⎫
avrai ⎬ avuto   sarai ⎬ stato(a)
avrà ⎭   sarà ⎭

avremo ⎫   saremo ⎫
avreste ⎬ avuto   sarete ⎬ stati(e)
avranno ⎭   saranno ⎭

CONDITIONAL PERFECT (CONDIZIONALE PASSATO)

I would have had

avrei
avresti } avuto
avrebbe

avremmo
avreste } avuto
avrebbero

I would have been

sarei
saresti } stato(a)
sarebbe

saremmo
sareste } stati(e)
sarebbero

SUBJUNCTIVE MOOD (MODO CONGIUNTIVO *OR* SOGGIUNTIVO)

PRESENT PERFECT (PASSATO)

(that) I may have had

abbia
abbia } avuto
abbia

abbiamo
abbiate } avuto
abbiano

(that) I may have been

sia
sia } stato(a)
sia

siamo
siate } stati(e)
siano

PLUPERFECT (TRAPASSATO)

(that) I might (would) have had

avessi
avessi } avuto
avesse

avessimo
aveste } avuto
avessero

(that) I might (would) have been

fossi
fossi } stato(a)
fosse

fossimo
foste } stati(e)
fossero

REGULAR VERBS (VERBI REGOLARI)

I -are	II -ere	III -ire

INFINITIVE (INFINITO)

I -are	II -ere	III -ire
parlare *to speak*	**credere** *to believe*	**finire** *to finish*

PRESENT PARTICIPLE (GERUNDIO)

I -are	II -ere	III -ire
parlando *speaking*	**credendo** *believing*	**finendo** *finishing*

PAST PARTICIPLE (PARTICIPIO PASSATO)

I -are	II -ere	III -ire
parlato *spoken*	**creduto** *believed*	**finito** *finished*

SIMPLE TENSES (TEMPI SEMPLICI)

INDICATIVE MOOD (MODO INDICATIVO)

PRESENT (PRESENTE)

I speak, do speak, am speaking	*I believe, do believe, am believing*	*I finish, do finish, am finishing*
parlo	credo	finisco[1]
parli	credi	finisci
parla	crede	finisce
parliamo	crediamo	finiamo
parlate	credete	finite
parlano	credono	finiscono

IMPERFECT OR PAST DESCRIPTIVE (IMPERFETTO)

I was speaking, used to speak, spoke	*I was believing, used to believe, believed*	*I was finishing, used to finish, finished*
parlavo	credevo	finivo
parlavi	credevi	finivi
parlava	credeva	finiva
parlavamo	credevamo	finivamo
parlavate	credevate	finivate
parlavano	credevano	finivano

PAST ABSOLUTE (PASSATO REMOTO)

I spoke, did speak	*I believed, did believe*	*I finished, did finish*
parlai	credei	finii
parlasti	credesti	finisti
parlò	credè	finì
parlammo	credemmo	finimmo
parlaste	credeste	finiste
parlarono	crederono (credettero)	finirono

FUTURE (FUTURO)

I will speak	*I will believe*	*I will finish*
parlerò	crederò	finirò
parlerai	crederai	finirai

1. A majority of verbs ending in -ire are conjugated on the model of **finire.** Some verbs ending in -ire, however, do not include the -isc insert in the 1st, 2nd and 3rd persons singular and the 3rd person plural of the present indicative, the present subjunctive and the imperative. Among these verbs are: **dormire** (*to sleep*), **partire** (*to leave*), **seguire** (*to follow*), **sentire** (*to feel, to hear*), **servire** (*to serve*), and **vestire** (*to dress*). Thus **partire**, for example, would be conjugated in the present indicative: **parto, parti, parte, partiamo, partite, partono.** There is also a number of verbs which may be conjugated on either model. These include: **applaudire** (*to applaud*), **avvertire** (*to warn*), **convertire** (*to convert*) and **divertire** (*to amuse*).

parlerà	crederà	finirà
parleremo	crederemo	finiremo
parlerete	crederete	finirete
parleranno	crederanno	finiranno

CONDITIONAL (CONDIZIONALE PRESENTE)

I would speak	*I would believe*	*I would finish*
parlerei	crederei	finirei
parleresti	crederesti	finiresti
parlerebbe	crederebbe	finirebbe
parleremmo	crederemmo	finiremmo
parlereste	credereste	finireste
parlerebbero	crederebbero	finirebbero

IMPERATIVE (IMPERATIVO)[1]

speak	*believe*	*finish*
parla	credi	finisci[2]
parlate	credete	finite
parli (Lei)	creda (Lei)	finisca (Lei)
parlino (Loro)	credano (Loro)	finiscano (Loro)
parliamo (*let us speak*)	crediamo (*let us believe*)	finiamo (*let us finish*)

SUBJUNCTIVE MOOD (MODO CONGIUNTIVO)

PRESENT (PRESENTE)

(that) I may speak	*(that) I may believe*	*(that) I may finish*
parli	creda	finisca[3]
parli	creda	finisca
parli	creda	finisca
parliamo	crediamo	finiamo
parliate	crediate	finiate
parlino	credano	finiscano

IMPERFECT (IMPERFETTO)

(that) I might (would) speak	*(that) I might (would) believe*	*(that) I might (would) finish*
parlassi	credessi	finissi
parlassi	credessi	finissi
parlasse	credesse	finisse
parlassimo	credessimo	finissimo
parlaste	credeste	finiste
parlassero	credessero	finissero

1. Only the second person forms are true imperatives. The other three are subjunctive forms used as imperatives.
2. Verbs on the model of **partire** (footnote, p. 109) have the following imperative forms: **parti, partite, parta, partano, partiamo.**
3. Verbs on the model of **partire** (footnote, p. 109) are conjugated in the present subjunctive: **parta, parta, parta, partiamo, partiate, partano.**

COMPOUND TENSES (TEMPI COMPOSTI)

INDICATIVE MOOD (MODO INDICATIVO)

PRESENT PERFECT (PASSATO PROSSIMO)

I have spoken

ho
hai } parlato
ha

abbiamo
avete } parlato
hanno

I have believed

ho
hai } creduto
ha

abbiamo
avete } creduto
hanno

I have finished

ho
hai } finito
ha

abbiamo
avete } finito
hanno

PLUPERFECT (TRAPASSATO PROSSIMO)

I had spoken

avevo
avevi } parlato
aveva

avevamo
avevate } parlato
avevano

I had believed

avevo
avevi } creduto
aveva

avevamo
avevate } creduto
avevano

I had finished

avevo
avevi } finito
aveva

avevamo
avevate } finito
avevano

SECOND PLUPERFECT (TRAPASSATO REMOTO)

I had spoken

ebbi
avesti } parlato
ebbe

avemmo
aveste } parlato
ebbero

I had believed

ebbi
avesti } creduto
ebbe

avemmo
aveste } creduto
ebbero

I had finished

ebbi
avesti } finito
ebbe

avemmo
aveste } finito
ebbero

FUTURE PERFECT (FUTURO ANTERIORE)

I will have spoken

avrò
avrai } parlato
avrà

avremo
avrete } parlato
avranno

I will have believed

avrò
avrai } creduto
avrà

avremo
avrete } creduto
avranno

I will have finished

avrò
avrai } finito
avrà

avremo
avrete } finito
avranno

CONDITIONAL PERFECT (CONDIZIONALE PASSATO)

I would have spoken

avrei
avresti } parlato
avrebbe

I would have believed

avrei
avresti } creduto
avrebbe

I would have finished

avrei
avresti } finito
avrebbe

avremmo			avremmo			avremmo	
avreste	} parlato		avreste	} creduto		avreste	} finito
avrebbero			avrebbero			avrebbero	

SUBJUNCTIVE MOOD (MODO CONGIUNTIVO)

PRESENT PERFECT (PASSATO)

(that) I may
have spoken

(that) I may
have believed

(that) I may
have finished

abbia			abbia			abbia	
abbia	} parlato		abbia	} creduto		abbia	} finito
abbia			abbia			abbia	
abbiamo			abbiamo			abbiamo	
abbiate	} parlato		abbiate	} creduto		abbiate	} finito
abbiano			abbiano			abbiano	

PLUPERFECT (TRAPASSATO)

(that) I might (would)
  have spoken

(that) I might (would)
  have believed

(that) I might (would)
  have finished

avessi			avessi			avessi	
avessi	} parlato		avessi	} creduto		avessi	} finito
avesse			avesse			avesse	
avessimo			avessimo			avessimo	
aveste	} parlato		aveste	} creduto		aveste	} finito
avessero			avessero			avessero	

ORTHOGRAPHIC-CHANGING VERBS (VERBI CON CAMBIAMENTO ORTOGRAFICO)

Verbs of the first conjugation ending in **-care** or **-gare** have an **h** before **i** or **e** in order to preserve the hard **c** and **g** sounds of the infinitive. This occurs in the following tenses:

PRES. IND.	cerco, **cerchi**, cerca, **cerchiamo**, cercate, cercano
PRES. SUBJ.	**cerchi, cerchi, cerchi, cerchiamo, cerchiate, cerchino**
IMPERATIVE	cerca, **cerchi, cerchiamo**, cercate, **cerchino**
FUT.	**cercherò, cercherai, cercherà, cercheremo, cercherete, cercheranno**
COND.	**cercherei, cercheresti, cercherebbe, cercheremmo, cerchereste, cercherebbero**

Other frequently used verbs of this type are:

asciugare *to dry*	**moltiplicare** *to multiply*
dimenticare *to forget*	**nevicare** *to snow*
giocare *to play*	**pagare** *to pay*
impiegare *to employ*	**pescare** *to fish*
masticare *to chew*	**significare** *to mean*
	spiegare *to explain*

Verbs of the first conjugation ending in **-ciare** and **-giare** drop the **i** whenever it precedes **e** or **i**. This occurs in the following tenses:

PRES. IND.	comincio, **cominci**, comincia, cominciamo, cominciate, cominciano
PRES. SUBJ.	**cominci, cominci, cominci,** cominciamo, cominciate, **comincino**
IMPERATIVE	comincia, **cominci,** cominciamo, cominciate, **comincino**
FUT.	**comincerò, comincerai, comincerà, cominceremo, comincerete, cominceranno**
COND.	**comincerei, cominceresti, comincerebbe, cominceremmo, comincereste, comincerebbero**

Other frequently used verbs of the **-ciare** and **-giare** types are:

bruciare *to burn*	viaggiare *to travel*
lasciare *to leave*	mangiare *to eat*

IRREGULAR VERBS (VERBI IRREGOLARI)

Only the mood and tenses that have irregularities are given here. The verbs which are conjugated with **essere** are preceded by an asterisk (*).

The following verbs are irregular only in the past absolute (P.A.) and the past participle (P.P.):

accendere *to light, to turn on;* P.A. **accesi, accendesti** *etc.;* P.P. **acceso**
appendere *to hang (up);* P.A. **appesi, appendesti** *etc.;* P.P. **appeso**
aprire *to open;* P.A. **apersi** or **aprii, apristi** *etc.;* P.P. **aperto**
chiedere *to ask (for);* P.A. **chiesi, chiedesti** *etc.;* P.P. **chiesto**
chiudere *to close;* P.A. **chiusi, chiudesti** *etc.;* P.P. **chiuso**
conoscere *to know;* P.A. **conobbi, conoscesti** *etc.;* P.P. **conosciuto**
consistere *to consist;* P.A. **consistetti, consistesti** *etc.;* P.P. **consistito**
correre *to run;* P.A. **corsi, corresti** *etc.;* P.P. **corso**
costruire *to construct;* P.A. **costrussi** or **costruii, costruisti** *etc.;* P.P. **costrutto** or **costruito**
crescere *to grow;* P.A. **crebbi, crescesti** *etc.;* P.P. **cresciuto**
decidere *to decide;* P.A. **decisi, decidesti** *etc.;* P.P. **deciso**
dipingere *to paint;* P.A. **dipinsi, dipingesti** *etc.;* P.P. **dipinto**
discutere *to discuss;* P.A. **discussi, discutesti** *etc.;* P.P. **discusso**
distinguere *to distinguish;* P.A. **distinsi, distinguesti** *etc.;* P.P. **distinto**
dividere *to divide;* P.A. **divisi, dividesti** *etc.;* P.P. **diviso**
escludere *to exclude:* P.A. **esclusi, escludesti** *etc.;* P.P. **escluso**
esprimere *to express;* P.A. **espressi, esprimesti** *etc.;* P.P. **espresso**
fondere *to melt;* P.A. **fusi, fondesti** *etc.;* P.P. **fuso**
*giungere *to arrive;* P.A. **giunsi, giungesti** *etc.;* P.P. **giunto**
leggere *to read;* P.A. **lessi, leggesti** *etc.;* P.P. **letto**
mettere *to put;* P.A. **misi, mettesti** *etc.;* P.P. **messo**
*nascere *to be born;* P.A. **nacqui, nascesti** *etc.;* P.P. **nato**
offrire *to offer;* P.A. **offersi** or **offrii, offristi** *etc.;* P.P. **offerto**
perdere *to lose;* P.A. **persi** or **perdei** or **perdetti, perdesti** *etc.;* P.P. **perso** or **perduto**
persuadere *to persuade;* P.A. **persuasi, persuadesti** *etc.;* P.P. **persuaso**
prendere *to take;* P.A. **presi, prendesti** *etc.;* P.P. **preso**
proteggere *to protect;* P.A. **protessi, proteggesti** *etc.;* P.P. **protetto**
radere *to shave;* P.A. **rasi, radesti** *etc.;* P.P. **raso**
rendere *to render;* P.A. **resi, rendesti** *etc.;* P.P. **reso**
ridere *to laugh;* P.A. **risi, ridesti** *etc.;* P.P. **riso**
rispondere *to answer;* P.A. **risposi, rispondesti** *etc.;* P.P. **risposto**
rompere *to break;* P.A. **ruppi, rompesti** *etc.;* P.P. **rotto**
*scendere *to descend;* P.A. **scesi, scendesti** *etc.;* P.P. **sceso**

scrivere *to write;* P.A. scrissi, scrivesti *etc.;* P.P. scritto

*sorgere *to arise, to flow from;* P.A. sorsi, sorgesti *etc.;* P.P. sorso

spendere *to spend;* P.A. spesi, spendesti *etc.;* P.P. speso

spingere *to push;* P.A. spinsi, spingesti *etc.;* P.P. spinto

*succedere *to happen (impersonal);* P.A. successe; P.P. successo

uccidere *to kill;* P.A. uccisi, uccidesti *etc.;* P.P. ucciso

vincere *to win;* P.A. vinsi, vincesti *etc.;* P.P. vinto

The following verbs have irregular forms in the tenses and moods indicated:

*accadere *to happen (impersonal)*

PAST ABS.	accadde
FUT.	accadrà

*andare *to go*

PRES. IND.	vado *or* vo, vai, va, andiamo, andate, vanno
FUT.	andrò, andrai, andrà, andremo, andrete, andranno
PRES. SUBJ.	vada, vada, vada, andiamo, andiate, vadano
IMPERATIVE	va', vada, andiamo, andate, vadano

*apparire *to appear*

PRES. IND.	appaio *or* apparisco, appari *or* apparisci, appare *or* apparisce, appariamo, apparite, appaiono *or* appariscono
PAST ABS.	apparsi *or* apparvi *or* apparii, apparisti, apparve *or* apparì, apparimmo, appariste, apparvero *or* apparirono
PRES. SUBJ.	appaia *or* apparisca, appaia *or* apparisca, appaia *or* apparisca, appariamo, appariate, appaiano *or* appariscano
IMPERATIVE	appari *or* apparisci, appaia *or* apparisca, appariamo, apparite, appaiano *or* appariscano
PAST PART.	apparso *or* apparito

bere *to drink*

PRES. IND.	bevo, bevi, beve, beviamo, bevete, bevono
PAST ABS.	bevvi *or* bevetti, bevesti, bevve, bevemmo, beveste, bevvero
FUT.	berrò, berrai, berrà, berremo, berrete, berranno
PRES. SUBJ.	beva, beva, beva, beviamo, beviate, bevano
IMPERATIVE	bevi, beva, beviamo, bevete, bevano
PRES. PART.	bevendo

*cadere *to fall*

PAST ABS.	caddi, cadesti, cadde, cademmo, cadeste, caddero
FUT.	cadrò, cadrai, cadrà, cadremo, cadrete, cadranno

cogliere *to gather.* (Also on this model: **raccogliere** *to gather, to pick up.*)

PRES. IND.	colgo, cogli, coglie, cogliamo, cogliete, colgono
PAST ABS.	colsi, cogliesti, colse, cogliemmo, coglieste, colsero
PRES. SUBJ.	colga, colga, colga, cogliamo, cogliate, colgano
IMPERATIVE	cogli, colga, cogliamo, cogliete, colgano
PAST PART.	colto

condurre *to conduct, to lead, to drive.* (Also on this model: **dedurre** *to deduct;* **tradurre** *to translate.*)

PRES. IND.	conduco, conduci, conduce, conduciamo, conducete, conducono
PAST ABS.	condussi, conducesti, condusse, conducemmo, conduceste, condussero
FUT.	condurrò, condurrai, condurrà, condurremo, condurrete, condurranno
PRES. SUBJ.	conduca, conduca, conduca, conduciamo, conduciate, conducano
IMPERF. SUBJ.	conducessi, conducessi, conducesse, conducessimo, conduceste, conducessero
IMPERATIVE	conduci, conduca, conduciamo, conduciate, conducano
PAST PART.	condotto
PRES. PART.	conducendo

cuocere *to cook*

PRES. IND.	cuocio, cuoci, cuoce, cociamo, cocete, cuociono
PAST ABS.	cossi, cocesti, cosse, cocemmo, coceste, cossero
PRES. SUBJ.	cuocia, cuocia, cuocia, cociamo, cociate, cuociano
IMPERATIVE	cuoci, cuocia, cociamo, cocete, cuociano
PAST PART.	cotto

dare *to give*

PRES. IND.	do, dai, da, diamo, date, danno
PAST ABS.	diedi *or* detti, desti, diede *or* dette, demmo, deste, diedero *or* dettero
FUT.	darò, darai, darà, daremo, darete, daranno
PRES. SUBJ.	dia, dia, dia, diamo, diate, diano
IMPERATIVE	da', dia, diamo, date, diano
PAST PART.	dato

dire *to say, to tell*

PRES. IND.	dico, dici, dice, diciamo, dite, dicono
PAST ABS.	dissi, dicesti, disse, dicemmo, diceste, dissero
FUT.	dirò, dirai, dirà, diremo, direte, diranno
PRES. SUBJ.	dica, dica, dica, diciamo, diciate, dicano
IMPERATIVE	di', dica, diciamo, dite, dicano
PAST PART.	detto
PRES. PART.	dicendo

dovere *to have to, must*

PRES. IND.	devo *or* debbo, devi, deve, dobbiamo, dovete, devono *or* debbono
FUT.	dovrò, dovrai, dovrà, dovremo, dovrete, dovranno
PRES. SUBJ.	deva *or* debba, deva *or* debba, deva *or* debba, dobbiamo, dobbiate, devano

fare *to do, to make*

PRES. IND.	faccio *or* fo, fai, fa, facciamo, fate, fanno
IMPERF. IND.	facevo, facevi, faceva, facevamo, facevate, facevano
PAST ABS.	feci, facesti, fece, facemmo, faceste, fecero
FUT.	farò, farai, farà, faremo, farete, faranno
PRES. SUBJ.	faccia, faccia, faccia, facciamo, facciate, facciano
IMPERATIVE	fa', faccia, facciamo, fate, facciano
PAST PART.	fatto
PRES. PART.	facendo

*morire *to die*

PRES. IND.	muoio, muori, muore, moriamo, morite, moiono
FUT.	morirò, *or* morrò, morirai, morirà, moriremo, morirete, moriranno
PRES. SUBJ.	muoia, muoia, muoia, moriamo, moriate, muoiano
PAST PART.	morto

muovere *to move*

PRES. IND.	muovo, muovi, muove, moviamo, movete, muovono
PAST ABS.	mossi, movesti, mosse, movemmo, moveste, mossero
PRES. SUBJ.	muova, muova, muova, moviamo, moviate, muovano
IMPERATIVE	muovi, muova, moviamo, movete, muovano
PAST PART.	mosso

*parere *to seem, to appear*

PRES. IND.	paio, pari, pare, paiamo, parete, paiono
PAST ABS.	parvi, paresti, parve, paremmo, pareste, parvero
FUT.	parrò, parrai, parrà, parremo, parrete, parranno
PRES. SUBJ.	paia, paia, paia, paiamo, pariate, paiano
PAST PART.	parso

*piacere *to please*

PRES. IND.	piaccio, piaci, piace, piaciamo *or* piacciamo, piacete, piacciono
PAST ABS.	piacqui, piacesti, piacque, piacemmo, piaceste, piacquero
PRES. SUBJ.	piaccia, piaccia, piaccia, piaciamo, piaciate, piacciano
IMPERATIVE	piaci, piaccia, piaciamo, piacete, piacciano
PAST PART.	piaciuto

porre *to put, to place.* (Also on this model: **supporre** *to suppose;* **comporre** *to compose.*)

PRES. IND.	pongo, poni, pone, poniamo, ponete, pongono
PAST ABS.	posi, ponesti, pose, ponemmo, poneste, posero
FUT.	porrò, porrai, porrà, porremo, porrete, porranno
PRES. SUBJ.	ponga, ponga, ponga, poniamo, ponete, pongano
IMPERATIVE	poni, ponga, poniamo, ponete, pongano
PAST PART.	posto

potere *to be able, can*

PRES. IND.	posso, puoi, può, possiamo, potete, possono
FUT.	potrò, potrai, potrà, potremo, potrete, potranno
PRES. SUBJ.	possa, possa, possa, possiamo, possiate, possano

*rimanere *to remain*

PRES. IND.	rimango, rimani, rimane, rimaniamo, rimanete, rimangono
PAST ABS.	rimasi, rimanesti, rimase, rimanemmo, rimaneste, rimasero
FUT.	rimarrò, rimarrai, rimarrà, rimarremo, rimarrete, rimarranno
PRES. SUBJ.	rimanga, rimanga, rimanga, rimaniamo, rimaniate, rimangano
IMPERATIVE	rimani, rimanga, rimaniamo, rimanete, rimangano
PAST PART.	rimasto

*salire *to ascend, to climb*

PRES. IND.	salgo, sali, sale, saliamo, salite, salgono
PRES. SUBJ.	salga, salga, salga, saliamo, saliate, salgano
IMPERATIVE	sali, salga, saliamo, salite, salgano

sapere *to know*

PRES. IND.	so, sai, sa, sappiamo, sapete, sanno
PAST ABS.	seppi, sapesti, seppe, sapemmo, sapeste, seppero
FUT.	saprò, saprai, saprà, sapremo, saprete, sapranno
PRES. SUBJ.	sappia, sappia, sappia, sappiamo, sappiate, sappiano
IMPERATIVE	sappi, sappia, sappiamo, sappiate, sappiano

scegliere *to choose, to select*

PRES. IND.	scelgo, scegli, sceglie, scegliamo, scegliete, scelgono
PAST ABS.	scelsi, scegliesti, scelse, scegliemmo, sceglieste, scelsero
PRES. SUBJ.	scelga, scelga, scelga, scegliamo, scegliate, scelgano
IMPERATIVE	scegli, scelga, scegliamo, scegliate, scelgano
PAST PART.	scelto

sciogliere *to untie, to melt*

PRES. IND.	sciolgo, sciogli, scioglie, sciogliamo, sciogliete, sciolgono
PAST ABS.	sciolsi, sciogliesti, sciolse, sciogliemmo, scioglieste, sciolsero
PRES. SUBJ.	sciolga, sciolga, sciolga, sciogliamo, sciogliate, sciolgano
IMPERATIVE	sciogli, sciolga, sciogliamo, sciogliete, sciolgano
PAST PART.	sciolto

sedere *to sit*

PRES. IND.	siedo *or* seggo, siedi, siede, sediamo, sedete, siedono *or* seggono
PRES. SUBJ.	segga, segga, segga, sediamo, sediate, siedano *or* seggano
IMPERATIVE	siedi, segga, sediamo, sedete, seggano

sottrarre *to subtract*

PRES. IND.	sottraggo, sottrai, sottrae, sottraiamo, sottraete, sottraggono
PAST ABS.	sottrassi, sottraesti, sottrasse, sottraemmo, sottraeste, sottrassero
FUT.	sottrarrò, sottrarrai, sottrarrà, sottrarremo, sottrarrete, sottrarranno
PRES. SUBJ.	sottragga, sottragga, sottragga, sottraiamo, sottraiate, sottraggano
IMPERATIVE	sottrai, sottragga, sottraiamo, sottraete, sottraggano
PAST PART.	sottratto

spegnere *to extinguish*

PRES. IND.	spengo, spengi, spenge, spengiamo, spengete, spengono
PAST ABS.	spensi, spengesti, spense, spengemmo, spengeste, spensero
PAST PART.	spento

*stare *to stay, to stand, to be*

PRES. IND.	sto, stai, sta, stiamo, state, stanno

PAST ABS.	stetti, stesti, stette, stemmo, steste, stettero
FUT.	starò, starai, starà, staremo, starete, staranno
PRES. SUBJ.	stia, stia, stia, stiamo, stiate, stiano
IMPERATIVE	sta', stia, stiamo, state, stiano

tenere *to hold, to have*

PRES. IND.	tengo, tieni, tiene, teniamo, tenete, tengono
PAST ABS.	tenni, tenesti, tenne, tenemmo, teneste, tennero
FUT.	terrò, terrai, terrà, terremo, terrete, terranno
PRES. SUBJ.	tenga, tenga, tenga, teniamo, teniate, tengano
IMPERATIVE	tieni, tenga, teniamo, tenete, tengano

togliere *to take from*

PRES. IND.	tolgo, togli, toglie, togliamo, togliete, tolgono
PAST ABS.	tolsi, togliesti, tolse, togliemmo, toglieste, tolsero
PRES. SUBJ.	tolga, tolga, tolga, togliamo, togliate, tolgano
IMPERATIVE	togli, tolga, togliamo, togliete, tolgano
PAST PART.	tolto

udire *to hear*

PRES. IND.	odo, odi, ode, udiamo, udite, odono
PRES. SUBJ.	oda, oda, oda, udiamo, udiate, odano
IMPERATIVE	odi, oda, udiamo, udite, odano

*uscire *to go out*

PRES. IND.	esco, esci, esce, usciamo, uscite, escono
PRES. SUBJ.	esca, esca, esca, usciamo, usciate, escano
IMPERATIVE	esci, esca, usciamo, uscite, escano

*valere *to be worth*

PRES. IND.	valgo, vali, vale, valiamo, valete, valgono
PAST ABS.	valsi, valesti, valse, valemmo, valeste, valsero
FUT.	varrò, varrai, varrà, varremo, varrete, varranno
PRES. SUBJ.	valga, valga, valga, valiamo, valiate, valgano
PAST PART.	valso

vedere *to see*

PAST ABS.	vidi, vedesti, vide, vedemmo, vedeste, videro
FUT.	vedrò, vedrai, vedrà, vedremo, vedrete, vedranno
PAST PART.	visto *or* veduto

*venire *to come*

PRES. IND.	vengo, vieni, viene, veniamo, venite, vengono
PAST ABS.	venni, venisti, venne, venimmo, veniste, vennero
FUT.	verrò, verrai, verrà, verremo, verrete, verranno
PRES. SUBJ.	venga, venga, venga, veniamo, veniate, vengano
IMPERATIVE	vieni, venga, veniamo, venite, vengano
PAST PART.	venuto

vivere *to live* (May be conjugated with either **essere** or **avere**.)

PAST ABS.	vissi, vivesti, visse, vivemmo, viveste, vissero
FUT.	vivrò, vivrai, vivrà, vivremo, vivrete, vivranno
PAST PART.	vissuto

volere *to will, to wish, to want*

PRES. IND.	voglio, vuoi, vuole, vogliamo, volete, vogliono
PAST ABS.	volli, volesti, volle, volemmo, voleste, vollero
FUT.	vorrò, vorrai, vorrà, vorremo, vorrete, vorranno
PRES. SUBJ.	voglia, voglia, voglia, vogliamo, vogliate, vogliano

NUMBERS (NUMERI)

CARDINALI

0	zero	30	trenta
1	uno, un, una	31	trentuno, trentun, trentuna
2	due	33	trentatrè
3	tre	40	quaranta
4	quattro	50	cinquanta
5	cinque	60	sessanta
6	sei	70	settanta
7	sette	80	ottanta
8	otto	90	novanta
9	nove	100	cento
10	dieci	101	centuno
11	undici	102	centodue
12	dodici	200	duecento
13	tredici	300	trecento
14	quattordici	400	quattrocento
15	quindici	500	cinquecento
16	sedici	600	seicento
17	diciasette	700	settecento
18	diciotto	800	ottocento
19	diciannove	900	novecento
20	venti	1.000	mille
21	ventuno, ventun, ventuna	1.001	mille uno
22	ventidue	2.000	duemila
23	ventitrè	5.888	cinquemila ottocento ottantotto
24	ventiquattro	27.777	ventisette mila settecento settanta-sette
25	venticinque		
26	ventisei	100.000	centomila
27	ventisette	1.000.000	un milione
28	ventotto	2.000.000	due milioni
29	ventinove	4.196.234	quattro milioni cento novantasei mila duecento trentaquattro

ORDINALI

1st	primo	6th	sesto
2nd	secondo	7th	settimo
3rd	terzo	8th	ottavo
4th	quarto	9th	nono
5th	quinto	10th	decimo